PLANTS & GARDENS
BROOKLYN BOTANIC GARDEN RECORD

This Handbook is a Special Revised Edition of PLANTS & GARDENS, Vol. 9, No. 3

DWARFED POTTED TREES
CONTENTS

I0359493

Editorial Staff for this is
KAN YASHIRODA, *Guest Editor*
With GEORGE S. AVERY, and the Editorial Committee of the Brooklyn Botanic Garden
Except where otherwise credited, photographs furnished by KAN YASHIRODA
NANCY M. TIM, *Circulation Manager*
DONALD E. MOORE, *President, Brooklyn Botanic Garden*
ELIZABETH SCHOLTZ, *Vice President, Brooklyn Botanic Garden*

Plants and Gardens, Brooklyn Botanic Garden Record (ISSN 0362-5850) is published quarterly at 1000 Washington Ave., Brooklyn, N.Y. 11225, by the **Brooklyn Botanic Garden, Inc.** Second-class-postage paid at Brooklyn, N.Y., and at additional mailing offices. Subscription included in Botanic Garden membership dues ($20.00 per year), which includes newsletters and announcements. Copyright © 1953, 1988 by the Brooklyn Botanic Garden, Inc.
    POSTMASTER: Send address changes to BROOKLYN BOTANIC GARDEN, Brooklyn, N.Y. 11225

An old but miniature forest of Yeddo spruce (*Picea jezoensis*)

Letter from the
Brooklyn Botanic Garden

Trees that grow in the rocky crevices of high mountains may live for a century or more, yet remain dwarfed throughout their existence. Windblown and often gnarled and twisted, their weather-buffeted appearance captures our interest and respect just as it caught the fancy of the Japanese long ago. Such trees are worthy of special appreciation, for their life struggle against adversity brings out qualities rarely seen in large trees at lower elevations. When grown in appropriate pots or containers, they become a form of living art that everyone interested in nature can understand. These dwarfed potted trees are the long-famous "bonsai" of Japan: they are "cultural dwarfs," not dwarf by heredity.

This Handbook tells how to train seedlings, cuttings and young nursery-grown trees so that in a few years they may assume the appearance of trees dwarfed by nature.

The word bonsai, literally translated, means "tray planting." I am told that it appears in Japanese writings only within the past century, even though the practice of growing such trees goes back many hundreds of years. In common with all nouns in the Japanese language, there is no distinction between singular and plural. Thus, one specimen is a bonsai, or many are bonsai. And the word is pronounced "bone-sigh," not "bon-zi."

Bonsai are not the artificially made "Ming Trees" of the florist shops; they are living trees that demand a certain amount of attention and affection. And the extent of ultimate perfection depends upon the skill and patience of the owner.

Bear in mind the viewing qualities of different bonsai at various times during the year: Some woody species make bonsai that retain their foliage and look much the same the year around (pine, juniper, spruce, etc.) Species that lose their leaves (deciduous kinds) may be prized during the winter months for the "architecture" of their trunks and branches. Japanese maple and gray-barked elm (pp. 40 and 41) are examples. Still others may retain their small bright-colored fruits for several weeks during the autumn, such as the crab apple (p. 57). Most bonsai that are prized for their flowers have only a short period of bloom. It is these seasonal qualities that make a varied bonsai collection one of unending interest.

For a list of species that make good bonsai, see the inside back cover of this Handbook. In general, the best trees or shrubs to use are those with small leaves, flowers and fruits. Those that develop good-sized trunks are especially prized.

It has been a great pleasure for members of our Editorial Committee to work with Guest Editor Yashiroda and his fellow countrymen on this bonsai Handbook. It is Mr. Yashiroda who has bridged the gap of language to bring English-speaking readers this authoritative account. While this is a revised edition, virtually all the original content remains. New material has been added to answer questions that have been put to us by the hundreds of students who have taken bonsai courses here at the Botanic Garden.

George S. Avery

Director Emeritus

One of the old timers, a Sargent juniper (*Juniperus chinensis sargenti*). It was leading a quiet life on a snowy mountain slope when found by an old man, Tahei, who took it from its native home more than a century ago. Its destiny was to spend whatever remained of its 800 to a thousand years as a bonsai, in a traditional container.

DWARFED POTTED TREES OR BONSAI

Their Culture and Use in Japan

Kan Yashiroda

WHEN I was invited to write on dwarfed potted trees or Bonsai, I could not help recalling a British broadcasting talk in which the speaker told us ". . . the Japanese love etiquette, formality and ceremoney of all kinds, and to the average American such things are poppycock." An American Army Colonel once informed me that the purpose behind the Noh plays, the tea ceremony and flower arrangement was simply to waste time. In that view, Bonsai should be in the same category. I fully admit that there may be some truth in it, though I have a different view.

The giant Sequoia (*Sequoia gigantea*) of the Sierras, having a beautiful, sturdy pyramidal shape when young—for the first hundred or more years; or the Yeddo Spruce* (*Picea jezoensis*) of Ezo attaining more than one hundred feet with picturesque branches, or the pure virgin forest of *Cryptomeria japonica* at Yanase silhouetting perfect form and luxury on the distant sky, are certainly, as G. K. Chesterton has said, "Unique shapes that an artist would copy or a philosopher watch for years." Japanese gardeners were greatly moved by the impressiveness of treedom, and it was the desire to copy trees in miniature shapes in their gardens and pots that produced dwarfed potted trees.

HISTORY

The history of the cultivation and appreciation of Bonsai is a very long one. The material used is almost boundless as to variety of plants and is no longer limited to the woody kinds only. Whether they are woody plants or herbaceous, dwarfing without hurting their natures, and keeping or modeling the vividness of Nature's own, are first objects in selecting and training of the material. The finished Bonsai should be roughly classified into three groups   naturally dwarfed plants; artificially dwarfed plants; dwarfed plants raised from seedlings and cuttings. Limiting myself to trees and shrubs, including conifers, I will touch on the three classes.

NATURALLY DWARFED TREES

On rocky crevices of high mountains, on perpendicular cliffs of tiny islands, on wettish bogs, and on the poorest and driest mountain slopes, some trees have lived through bravely for almost a century, or more, only growing a few feet high, panting and straining under the pressure of hard weather. Some of these

* Although called *Yeddo* Spruce in America, this name is erroneous. In Japan it is called *Ezo Matsu*, after its habitat Ezo—which is the island now called Hokkaido. *Yeddo* is the old name of Tokyo.

trees are worthy of our appreciation of their dwarfed but stout trunks, and weather-beaten picturesque branches. The notable examples are Sargent Juniper (*Juniperus chinensis sargenti*) of Iyo and Echigo Provinces, Japanese Black Pine (*Pinus thunbergi*) of Shodoshima, Yeddo spruce of Hokkaido and the Kurile Islands, and the rhododendrons *obtusum* and *kiusianum* of Kyushu.

Sargent Juniper dwells on high perpendicular cliffs, not accessible by climbing; however, nearly all the noted habitats are now barren of material as it was collected wantonly by the professional collectors. When I was a boy, nice naturally dwarfed trees were found, many on Mt. Ishizuchi of Iyo Province. A professional collector once told me a story of the toil and superstition of his collecting, which will well illustrate how such collecting is done for a livelihood. By his keen eyes or with the aid of a field-glass, from far beneath on the cliff, he first finds a nice tree—which often may vanish into the fog above. He then seeks a suitable spot near the edge of the cliff where he may sleep for the night. Next, he draws a circle some six feet in diameter, and stands on the edge of it, He takes off his upper cloth, or working coat, and places it within the circle, facing toward him. The coat is a substitute for his Deity, and he places grains of rice before it as an offering. Then he prays solemnly, "I am a dwarf tree collector by profession. Please let me rent the spot for the night." After the prayer is done, feeling that he will not encounter or meet with mischief from long-nosed goblins or monsters, he rests for the night.

In the morning he ties firmly one end of a rope to a tree trunk on the cliff's edge and the other end to his body. Holding the coiled ropes and tools such as hammer and chisel, which are used to remove the roots from the rock, and with saw, scissors and knife, he gratefully works his way downward to the tree, moving along the cliff. Often the tree is growing on the concave part of the cliff.

5

Mitsukoshi Exhibition

Kurume azalea

perhaps underneath a protruding rock; in such cases he lowers himself by the rope to the nearby desired dwarf tree, and then swinging himself, he patiently awaits a chance to grasp the tree or the cliff nearby where he can reach the tree. The digging is a most patient and laborious work, taking many hours. Roughly describing his routine of work, the old timer had frightened me, telling, with an exaggerated gesture, how, had he not prayed, the goblin or monster might come and untie the rope while he worked on the cliff below. Oh! the good old timer is dead long ago, but whenever I recall him I recall the poem "The Last Leaf," by Oliver Wendell Holmes. Perhaps he should be called, fittingly, one of the "last leaves" in his orthodox faith and way. Good, kindly and genial man he was. It is possible that the Sargent's

Juniper in the photograph is one of the trees he had collected on Mt. Ishizuchi.

Sargent Junipers growing on rocky cliffs are much dwarfed and of artistic beauty so need only a little training if any is necessary. But as they are taken bare-rooted and roughly from rocky places, they should later be given great care. They are planted and cared for two or more years in specially prepared beds, and at the same time are trained to the desired shape. Foliage is thinned if necessary. When well rooted, and the trained branches are fixed, the trees should be placed in pottery containers. This is how naturally dwarfed trees are prepared.

Another much appreciated tree which is found growing naturally in extremely dwarfed form is Yeddo Spruce. It inhabits wettish bogs where exposed to severe wind and cold. It is hard even for the expert to realize that other Yeddo spruces growing not for from the bog, some of them attaining a height of one hundred feet or more, are the same species. On sunny mountain slopes where the residual soil is poor and thin, Needle Junipers (*Juniperus rigida*) are found a few inches high—with crooked trunks and picturesque foliage (on which waxy, globular fruits hang in decoration). The same region produces, also nearly naturally dwarfed Japanese Black and Red Pines. But nowadays such naturally occurring ones are rarely discovered. Sargent Juniper, Japanese Black Pine and Yeddo Spruce are the big three among the dwarfed trees; these are extensively grown and appreciated in Japan. But owing to the demand, and because naturally dwarfed trees are limited in supply and very expensive, artificially dwarfed trees are also much cultivated.

ARTIFICIALLY DWARFED TREES

The majority of the dwarfed potted trees generally seen are developed from ordinary nursery stock or from somewhat dwarfed trees found in a natural habitat. The practice of artificial dwarfing might be more aptly described as "revolutionizing" normal growth. What, then, is this practice?

Ordinary Nursery Stock

Let me first take some examples of the ordinary nursery stock, and tell about them. Three- to ten-year-old young trees of the following are suitable for "revolutionizing":

Evergreens: Japanese White Pine (*Pinus parviflora*), Japanese Larch (*Larix kaempferi* (*L. leptolepis*)), Hinoki Cypress (*Chamaecyparis obtusa*), and such conifers as are grown in nurseries for ordinary garden purposes or for forest plantations.

Deciduous: Japanese Maple (*Acer palmatum* and varieties), *Daphne odora*,

flowering Peach (*Prunus persica* varieties), Japanese flowering Apricot (*Prunus mume* varieties), Japanese flowering Quince (*Chaenomeles lagenaria*), garden varieties of Hall's flowering Crabapple (*Malus halliana*). Such ornamental trees and shrubs have trunks and branches that are comparatively easy to bend. They are taken from nurseries in autumn, and potted. A small pot is preferred to accustom the plant to the smaller space for root development and to restrain the growth of foliage. However, when selecting the pot, consider its depth; the shallower the pot, the better the result, but it should be of fairly generous width. When the trees are started on their way to dwarfing, they are generally planted in shallow containers, as they look better and seem to have a more aesthetic touch.

In late winter or early spring, possibly while drinking tea, you begin to fancy the shape of the tree when finished. The man experienced in training with wire changes ordinary little trees into different forms almost instantly, sometimes to a shape seen in naturally dwarfed trees. The wiring specialist's way is about like this: in the autumn the tree should have been potted so that the trunk is inclined to slant. Then in spring, to shorten the trunk in height and lower the branches, a wire is fastened to the trunk near the surface of the soil in the pot, and again attached higher up so the trunk can be pulled downward, away from the direction of the slant. It should be fastened at the desired bend with the wire. After the operation the little tree will have been considerably lowered, and then another wire is fastened at the forked part, the end of the wire coiling around the trunk; carefully wind the wire toward the tip, having an inch or more in intervals of the spiral. The branch is then ready to be shaped and fixed to the desired form. The second upper branch is treated in the same way, then the third, and so on. After one or two years, in many cases, the trunk and branches should be settled in the desired positions,

7

so the winding wires are no longer needed, and may be taken off. From year to year the tree is improved in form and foliage as the result of careful pinching of certain tip buds, shortening or removing undesired strong shoots, repeating the pinching often in a season according to the kind of tree and further winding the wire to change the form or improve it. Gradually the artificial look lightens and the "made-up" tree becomes the natural-looking tree. The course of training for years is very fascinating to fanciers, novices and experts alike. It is not unusual in a day's stroll in the villages or towns in Japan, wherever you may be, to come across people who train dwarf trees—they are a set of cheerful boasters.

Ordinary stock of pines, daphnes, azaleas, maples and such ornamentals, when only one or two feet high, are often bent almost upside down, by wire-winding the trunk. Heavy copper wire is used. ranches are wound with lighter wire and bent so as to achieve the desired form. Whenever wiring is practiced, soil in the pot should be drier than usual so trunks and branches are easily worked. Copper wire of heavy gauge should be heated to red-heat, then cooled slowly before using. This makes it easier to bend. But beware. Once bent, it hardens again quickly. Some fanciers do not like to use wire, but the operation is not so shocking as vivisection and not as unnatural as "miniature" gardens sold in America— even though the trees have been completely "revolutionized." After a course of training and settling, the trees grow naturally and look natural; the chief difference is that they grow less rapidly than the ordinary nursery stock. But normal, healthy foliage is produced in tidier textures.

Collected Stock

Now we come to the second group, the trees brought from natural habitats. From mountains and ragged woods, a tremendous amount of material is dug and brought to the training beds of dwarfed potted trees specialists each year. There it remains for several years to be established, trained and finally "made-up."

In the case of naturally occurring, partially dwarfed trees, there is need only for a few wires and a little training. Trees that have lost the greater part of their roots are a more serious problem. Some of them die because of their inadequate root system, particularly if the first summer is hot and dry. To illustrate, I now describe the collection of Japanese Black Pine. On the mountain of Shodoshima or Shodo Island which is located in the Seto Inland Sea National Park a countless number of Japanese Black Pine for dwarfed potted trees have been dug by professional collectors. Many renowned and valuable dwarfed Black Pines were produced from the material collected here. I am writing this at my home which is situated at the foot of the Shodoshima Mountain. On the islet opposite my house a Black Pine was collected many years ago, which became the most precious and dearest of all dwarfed potted Black Pines. There are still some stories or legends circulated concerning it.

Seeing the spot through Bald Cypress (*Taxodium distichum*) and Cypress-Pine (*Callitris glauca*) in the Acclimatization Gardens as I am writing, I vividly recall the days when collectors came to the island in autumn and spring. The surface rock is granite. Higher up on the mountain the rocks weather into coarse whitish sand and the layer of soil is very thin; at lower levels there is a greater depth of soil and always some moisture. The district is one of the lowest in rainfall in Japan. The summer is very hot and almost bone dry. On the upper parts of both sides of the ridge, Black Pine dominates; next comes Red Pine (*Pinus densiflora*) and in far lesser numbers the Needle Juniper, *Rhododendron reticulatum*, *Rhododendron kaemferi*, Bush Clover (*Lespedeza bicolor*) and Balloon-flower (*Platycodon grandiflorum*). The pines are very dwarfed in

8

Kurume azaleas in full leaf—arranged for appreciation by bonsai fanciers

size but in most cases they are older than the larger ones seen at the lower levels on the mountain. Three feet is generally regarded as the maximum height of dwarfed potted trees. To keep within the golden rule of Bonsai, the larger trees are often sharply pruned. For example, on discovering a very dwarfed pine five or more feet in height with a trunk five or more inches in diameter, if the lower branches are three feet from the ground and picturesque in form (or promise to be so if trained), the upper portion of the main trunk is sawed off. It is important that when healed the cut surface should be inconspicuous. Undesirable branches are cut off. Then the digging begins. The trench is dug out carefully, cutting off all the roots outside a radius of a foot all the way around the tree, and to a depth of a foot or often less. Only the tap root remains uncut. First the straw rope is coiled cautiously and rather firmly thrice or more horizontally around the ball and then all around the surface of the ball,

so the very porous, coarse, sandy soil ball is firmly held about the roots; the tap root is finally sawed through, and the tree is removed You may wonder at the proportionately small size of the ball, but usually seventy per cent or more of the trees collected survive and become well settled as dwarfed potted trees; occasionally in very dry, hot summers, fifty per cent or so succumb. For such collected stock, training by wire is practiced generally after a year or two, when the plants are well established.

DWARFED TREES RAISED FROM SEEDLINGS AND CUTTINGS

One of the most fascinating hobbies is the raising of trees from seeds sown directly in a shallow container. If the seedlings are allowed to grow for a few years, they appear like a miniature forest; the same may be done with cuttings.

The following trees and shrubs may be sown directly in shallow containers

9

or boxes, less than four inches in depth; Japanese maples, birches, beeches, Pomegranate, Yeddo Spruce, pines and many other conifers; also Wex-Tree (*Rhus succedanea*), Lacquer-Tree (*Rhus verniciflua*), Maidenhair Tree (*Ginkgo biloba*), *Cryptomeria japonica*, *Ilex serrata* and *Zelkova serrata*. When the young seedlings are established they may be transplanted thickly to another shallow container or singly to a pot. The single planted ones in thumb pots should be shifted to slightly larger pits every two or three years. Two or three such transplantings should be enough.

Pinching

During the growing season pinching off growing tips should not be neglected—otherwise, whether seedlings or old dwarfs, the trees will be unsightly in form and disproportionately long branches will be produced. Generally, pinching is practiced and begins when young shoots are an inch or so long. Only one or two leaves are allowed to remain on any one branch. In the case of conifers such as spruces and pines, pinching should be done as the soft new branches elongate and begin to show their new needles. Every new twig should be pinched back, except the ones desired to improve form or to fill a gap; only a bit of elongated shoot should remain, from which the new buds are formed. Unsightly or deformed dwarfed potted trees, often seen at the novice's home, are in most cases the result of wrong pinching or neglect of pinching.

Densely twigged trees such as elm, maple, pomegranate and zelkova, should be pinched during the growing season whenever the twigs attain one or two inches in length. Always remember to retain one or two leaves on each branch.

The flowering shrubs such as azalea, enkianthus, rose, quince and jasmine, or fringe-tree and crabapple, contrary to the preceding, should not be pinched even lightly. Pinching back of these varieties removes the flower buds and prevents flowering.

The weeping willow and tamarix trained in weeping form are better if all the new twigs are cut off in the middle of spring. When new growth starts again, — the weeping branchlets that are produced will be more slender and delicate.

Varieties

Now, I feel it is better to select a few trees which would probably be of interest to readers and try to describe in a few words the essential points on their culture.

Flowering Cherries. Japanese flowering cherries are nicer as garden trees but sometimes well known garden varieties are attractive as dwarfed potted trees. In dwarfing these trees, the general practice is no pinching or pruning. Among the flowering cherries, the best is *Prunus incisa* and its varieties. This densely-twigged dwarf shrub is very lovely with little single blooms. *Prunus kurilensis* is good, too. Over-watering may kill the whole plant or destroy most of the branches.

Flowering Crabapples. Among these the most popular is Hall's Crabapple, known for nearly ninety years in American gardens. The tree is easily trained to one or two feet in height by bending or coiling the long shoots. So trained, these produce many flowering spurs and become very floriferous. Every spring the trees are a beautiful sight with their lovely rose-colored blooms hanging gracefully on long, slender, reddish flower stalks.

Fanciers love the aged trees of *Malus baccata* var. *hondoensis* with copious small bright fruits, *Malus prunifolia* and its varieties with yellow or red fruits, and *Malus sieboldi*, all of them known in American gardens for many years. If bushy growth is desired, all or nearly all the leaves on the current growth should be picked off in early summer; subsequently every axillary bud comes into growth. In the autumn the sprouted twigs are shortened to two or three buds.

Peaches and Pears. Though rarely

seen as dwarfed potted trees they make lovely ones. These and the preceding are, with afew exceptions, called by the "dignified" connoisseurs merely "potted ⁀owering trees"

Birches. By planting several very young seedlings a few inches high in a shallow container the shape of a rectangle or an ellipse (with a depth of two inches or more, and about one by two feet, or less) the beautiful scenes of a birch community are easily achieved in less than ten years. Every birch that attains one to two feet in height is limited and kept to that height easily, and needs only pinching to regulate growth. The dwarfed trees prossess the fine slender white-barked trunks, with handsome foliage. I highly recommend that you try birch. Place the container, in summer, into another larger and shallower basin filled with water and carry it to your room. It will be cheerful to both the birches and yourself.

Beeches, Elms and Zelkova. Raising these densely twigged trees from seedlings is fascinating, but requires patience. In the spring their tender young foliage is a delicate green. They are refreshing in form and color in summer, clear yellow in fall, and in winter they have above all, the enchanting form of pygmy giants. Their aged and exposed roots enhance and express the vividness of "giants" seen in nature. Unless they are pinched back very often during the growing season the trees do not shape-up well. Besides the pinching, it is advisable to cut off the leaves in early summer to hasten the development of denser twigs, Repotting should be done every other year. Some of the soil attached to the roots is shaken off and the roots thus exposed cut off. The new soil should have fertilizer but less sand than the usual potting mixture to prevent the dying off of twigs.

Maples. A tremendous number of various garden varieties of Japanese maple are propagated by inarching, trained as dwarfed trees, and sold an-

nually. Few plants are more refreshing than these maples in the hot Japanese summer. On verandas, in windows, in the alcove when guests are expected, on the office desk, in refreshment rooms, and by the side of lecturers, you will find the graceful foliage of these handsome miniature trees. If you like fall color and live where trees do not ordinarily display it, pick off all the leaves in early summer and you can be sure that the second growth of leaves will soon appear, and produce gorgeous colors. Repeated pinching is most needed.

Rhododendrons and Azaleas. One of the most popular dwarfed potted trees is the azalea. Among these, Satsuki and Kurume azaleas are extensively grown and enjoyed. There are hundreds of desirable varieties. Names of Japanese varieties will not be particularly helpful to bonsai fanciers in other countries. An important quality in rhododendron and azalea bonsai is the fact that they are evergreen. Only small-leaved and small-flowered varieties should be selected for training. As the flowers fade, or earlier,

An old collected plant of the five-needle pine (*Pinus parviflora*) in which the dead section of the trunk has been purposely kept to add character and a feeling of antiquity to the plant.

A 300-year-old specimen of azalea variety YOKIHI

undesirable twigs should be cut off or shortened. In the latter case the new growth, if crowded should be thinned. Young plants should be repotted once a year, but every two or three years is sufficient as they grow older. Nowadays, I regret to say, there is a fever for overwiring to hasten the production of dwarfed trees —and thus to fill the gap caused by the loss of old trees during the war. This is especially true for Satsuki azaleas, which are in fashion. To me, the resulting plants look as if they had been seized by wires. They are only artificially picturesque and old-looking.

Many nice naturally dwarfed rhododendrons are found and dug out annually. When well settled in containers they are very lovely, though not comparable in gorgeousness, and size of bloom to the modern hybrids. *Rhododendron obtusum* and *Rhododendron kiusianum* from which Kurume azaleas were derived, are desirable ones to grow as dwarfed potted trees.

Pines. Pines, the inhabitants of the poor, dry, sandy soils, become weakened or die off if the drainage is poor in the containers. But as pines are vigorous in their nature, the repotting is only necessary once in every three or four years. With deciduous trees it is generally better to repot each year. In either case, the best season for reporting is in the spring. If the pine tree is removed from the container, with its ball of soil, very long roots will be seen on the underside; these must be shortened rather severely. Some soil should be removed from all faces of the ball, and the exposed root and rootlets cut off. In repotting, put coarse sand sparingly on the bottom of the same container; place the pine on the sand and fill the container with new soil to take the place of the old (for full instructions on re-potting techniques, turn to page 24). For dwarfer and denser growth, the pinching, as previously referred to, must not be neglected. As the

Mountain slopes where soil is poor and thin frequently produce picturesque trees like this—
the inspiration for bonsai

tree becomes older the pinching should be lighter. The thickly cork-barked Black Pines are much admired for their trunks; the bark is thicker than the trunk itself. Japanese Red Pines are not much appreciated, but their slender trunks with impressive reddish bark are very ornamental—whether planted singly or several trees together in a container. It is more difficult for the average fancier to keep the branches and twigs of Red Pine healthy. The Japanese White Pine (*Pinus parviflora*) is extensively grown and dwarfed, though there are also many naturally dwarfed, aged trees of this species. Pines symbolize longevity.

Japanese Flowering Apricots. If you are in Japan in the midst of winter, you will see Japanese homes with flowering apricots (*Prunus mume*) in dwarfed potted forms. There are numerous named varieties, single flowered or semi-double, upright and weeping. These dwarfed potted Mumes bring life-long joy with their delightful and very sweet fragrant blooms in late winter and early spring. Just after the blooms have faded, every shoot or twig that bloomed should be shortened to the lowest one or two buds, from which new growth soon comes to replace the twigs that were removed.

Bamboo. The bamboos are dwarfed by peeling off the sheath, one a day, while the shoots are very young. The dwarfed potted bamboos are very decorative indoors and out.

Within the limits of this introductory article, I have tried to give readers something of the feeling of bonsai and the general methods used in their culture. Now please turn to the many special articles that follow!

OUSTANDING PLANTS FOR BONSAI

Hints on their culture and training

Y. Saida and M. Saida

Sargent Juniper

JUNIPERUS chinensis sargenti is one of the very popular bonsai. Practically all the old bonsai of this tree are developed from specimens taken from their natural habitats by professional collectors, from the northern part of the so-called Japan Alps in West Middle Japan, from Iyo Province, from Hokkaido, and from other places where the tree grows.

Cuttings. Young bonsai Sargent juniper are raised from cuttings. Young shoots 2 to 3 inches long are taken, the lower leaves are cut off, and the cut-tings are pared slightly on one side. These are inserted in a bed of clean sand in a coldframe, in the spring or in autumn. In a few years they are ready to be trained and trimmed as bonsai.

Training. Wiring is best done in early spring. Pinching and trimming are done in May and June. Care must be taken not to destroy the natural form of Sargent juniper, which is to have roundish compact growth on the main branches.

Fertilizer is given often in the spring and in the autumn; none in midsummer. A handful or rape cake or soy bean cake is placed on each of two or three spots on the soil in the container; or these fertilizers are fermented and applied in liquid form, greatly diluted. The liquid fertilizers are applied twice a week or so. See page 95 for guidance.

Sargent juniper does not need much water.

Japanese White Pine

Pinus parviflora is another very popular bonsai tree. Many professional collectors of bonsai material risk great danger to obtain naturally dwarfed specimens from high cliffs, ravines, and desolate high mountains where these trees are in eternal struggle with the ravaging elements. The collecting is done in Iyo Province of Shikoku, Echigo, Yamato, and in southern Japan.

Sargent juniper, a very popular plant for dwarfing

Mitsukoshi Exhibition

A three-trunked Japanese white pine. Tall slender bonsai in small shallow containers sometimes need a prop like the thin bamboo stick shown here.

If the soil is too rich, or if water is given liberally when the new growth is developing, the leaves become long and untidy.

It is necessary to pinch or cut off the new growth while it is young and soft, to maintain a shapely bonsai that will not be spindling. One may think the tall tree in the photograph is spindling and wonder if it became so because it was not pinched. The appearance of this tree is not the result of gradual dying of the branches from the lower to the upper, which is generally seen in trees poorly or wrongly treated and trained. This tree has been trained to this form from an artistic point of view, to achieve nearly parallel growth of three trunks.

The low and spreading Japanese white pine shown on the next page has several trunks from the soil. It is not several trees growing together but is a single tree; this form of bonsai is called *Netsuranari* and is very fashionable; the trunks and roots are connected.

Clasping a Stone

The Yeddo spruce shown on the next page and the Japanese white pine on page 17 are planted on stones—a style of bonsai tried by every bonsai fancier and called *Ishitsuki*, or plant clasping a stone.

In choosing a stone suitable for planting a tree or trees, several factors should be considered: for example, whether the stone has a concave surface in which the tree may be planted, and whether there are crevices in which the tree may be placed or along which the roots may be directed downward, finally to be anchored in a pocket in the stone or in the container. The stone must be stable in the container in all

15

A very shapely Japanese
white pine with five trunks

cases. Not less to be considered is the color of the stone, to harmonize with the tree planted on it and with the surroundings in which it is to be placed for display. For the good of the tree, somewhat soft stones are preferred, and in some cases kinds that absorb water.

In **planting trees on stones**, the novice is likely to use bigger and older trees, but that does not always bring

Yeddo spruce (*Picea jezoensis*) trained to a picturesque shape; growing on a weathered stone (Tufa rock lends itself to this use).

good results. Very young trees are far better to begin with. The roots of the bigger and older trees are rather stunted and do not spread well on the stone or grow down into the soil in the container; but the roots of the little young trees spread vigorously in every direction and grow well. In a few years the young trees overtake the older ones; but their growth is easily controlled and the trees kept dwarf because the trees themselves and most of their roots are on the stone.

The **container** in which the stone and tree are placed, with soil, is not a basin to hold water but is like the containers used for ordinary bonsai: it has holes in the bottom (generally two or so).

On the Yeddo spruce shown here on the stone, rather thick copper wires are coiled upward to bend the trunk; two are used on the lower part.

Miniature Forest

The miniature forest of Yeddo spruce (*Picea jezoensis*) shown on the opposite

16

A much-dwarfed Japanese white pine growing on a stone

page was created from one tree. The trunk of a young, well-branched tree was laid horizontally under the soil of the container. The bases of the branches were covered and their upper parts projected above the soil. In the course of years, roots came out from many parts of the buried trunk, and each branch became just like an independent trunk.

Japanese Zelkova

The photograph of *Zelkova serrata* (next page) shows the roots spreading on the surface, the same as in giant old trees; also the branches growing obliquely upward, as they do in old trees in nature. It is good taste to train the bonsai tree to be a model of the natural tree.

Pinching. As this tree grows well, and dense growth of twigs is much appreciated, repeated pinching of the young growth should not be neglected. If all the leaves are cut off in June, new

growth soon appears and becomes denser.

Soil. For other bonsai good drainage is essential; but if the soil for Japanese zelkova is too sandy, the branches are likely to die.

Fertilizers that are too strong encourage the growth of too vigorous shoots. Japanese zelkova is naturally a strong

Miniature forest of Yeddo spruce developed from one tree by the method described on page 85

17

The gray-barked elm (*Zelkova serrata*), a native of Japan, makes a shapely dwarfed tree. Exposed roots, as in this specimen, suggest that soil erosion has occurred, thus helping to convey the impression of old age.

grower and so should have only very dilute liquid fertilizer.

Repotting should be done every other year. The tree is taken out of the shallow container; some of the soil is removed from the sides and bottom of the old soil clump, and the roots that are thus exposed are cut off. The tree is then repotted in the container, with new soil to replace what was removed.

Japanese-creeper

Boston-ivy (*Parthenocissus tricuspidata*) is native to Japan and China. Our autumn tints are due to this ivy in many places, particularly on rocky cliffs, where it spreads thickly and clings firmly by tendrils with adhesive tips. It stands dust and soot well and so will make a good bonsai in the city. Although a climber in nature, it can easily be kept shrubby as wisteria can. The photograph shows how the plant should be trimmed.

Trident Maple

Maples are much appreciated for their young green foliage, for their autumn color, and in the winter for their well formed delicate branches, branchlets, and trunk.

Boston-ivy, or Japanese creeper, kept in a shrubby form and grown as bonsai.

18

Trident maple copse in late autumn after leaf fall. Roots creeping over rock give feeling of venerability. The tree responds well to culture as bonsai and displays good autumn color.

The trident maple (*Acer buergerianum,* or *A. trifidum*) was introduced into Japan from China centuries ago. It is the one most frequently seen as bonsai. Tremendous numbers are grown because it responds well to trimming, has a tendency to form roots on the surface of the soil, produces dense growth with vigorous small neat leaves which are pleasing when young and in autumn colors, and has other virtues. As it grows very vigorously, shooting up quickly here and there, pinching must not be neglected, and continually repeated pinching is necessary, leaving two leaves on each shoot.

On the maple and on some other trees, it is a common and well-worthwhile practice to cut off all the leaves in mid-summer, when young shoots are beginning to harden. If all the leaves are cut off, the tree soon produces new ones, which will show brighter autumn colors than the old ones would.

Repotting. It is important to repot a maple each spring, taking off the old soil carefully and cutting off most of the roots produced in the last year. Thus it will grow nicely, yet remain dwarf, in the same container for years. With the less vigorous maples, the roots are cut less.

19

E. Satomi

Japanese flowering cherries are considered difficult to train as bonsai. Shown above is one of the many varieties of *Prunus subhirtella.*

Flowering Cherries

Japanese flowering cherries are so well known as to call for only brief mention. They are grown abundantly everywhere in Japan, but it is very *rare* to come across them as bonsai. According to general opinion, they are among the most difficult trees to grow as bonsai, and this is strictly true except for a few experts who are always particularly fond of them.

Varieties. Many varieties are suitable for bonsai; only a few are not so good, such as KIRIN, with branches too stout, AMANOGAWA, with fastigiate growth, and a small number of others. There are many varieties familiar in foreign countries and better for bonsai, such as KWANZAN

20

A carefully trained specimen of Japanese flowering cherry

(SEKIYAMA), erect, with spreading branches and double deep rose-pink flowers; ITOKUKURI, with semidouble pale pink flowers prettily clustered; MURASAKI-ZAKURA, a nice slow grower with semidouble purplish pink flowers; HIZAKURA, the best grower, with lovely rose-pink flowers; *Prunus subhirtella pendula* [the weeping variety of rosebud cherry], with slender drooping branches; *P. subhirtella pendula plena rosea*, with flowers of deeper color; and the wild *P. serrulata spontanea*. Old dwarfed specimens of *P. incisa* are collected and grown as bonsai.

As Japanese flowering cherries bloom gorgeously and abundantly each year, they make the most colorful bonsai, if grown well. Varieties with smaller flowers make more attractive bonsai than those with larger flowers. Consistency of scale is important!

Training. I hasten to say that the burned copper wire so much used in the training of bonsai is taboo in the culture of Japanese flowering cherries; it should never be used in their training or put on them for any purpose. Anyone who ventures to use it on them finds that the branches soon die and consequently the tree becomes a sad sight.

The branches, roots, and rootlets must be cut very smoothly, with no ragged edges. Shears may be used; but some growers are careful to avoid using ordinary pruning shears and use Japanese razors and knives instead. If a root is damaged, it will die and rot just as quickly as a branch.

The curved trunk shown in the accompanying photograph was originally a side branch. It was carefully bent and

21

E. Satomi

Japanese flowering apricot is more frequently used for bonsai than flowering cherry. It is easier to train and the flowers are more in keeping with the dwarf size of the tree.

pulled down by means of a rope tied to it and fastened to the container when the branch was bent to the desired shape. The rope was kept on for months. A piece of cloth was placed on the branch where the rope touched it. Instead of cloth, hemp or Japanese paper or pieces of split bamboo are often used, for all kinds of bonsai; adhesive tape is harmful.

If three buds are formed at the tip of a branch, the middle one should be nipped off to make the tree grow as a dwarf and to prevent the dying of the smaller branches.

Repotting is best done in March, before the new growth starts. In repotting, very carefully wash off as much as possible of the old soil or as much as seems best for the tree. Cut off smoothly any rotten roots and some of the older ones. If, for one reason or another, you cut off a lot of the roots, be careful to reduce the branches in proportion, to keep the roots and top in balance.

The soil used is very porous; we bring it from the mountains. Stagnant water kills the roots of cherry tree bonsai and causes the plants to die.

Fertilizers are applied as to other bonsai—rape cake and the like.

Pests. Just as we favor flowering cherries, the insects are very fond of them, both in the air and in the soil. Beware of these.

Japanese Flowering Apricot

Prunus mume is a popular flowering tree for bonsai. Plants that are too floriferous or too gorgeously colored are rather avoided for bonsai. Japanese flowering apricot is not so gorgeous, however, as flowering cherries and flowering quinces.

In flowering apricot bonsai the Japanese appreciate particularly the aged trunk and the one-year-old shoots fresh in pleasing green. When the flowering season comes, we like to have some blossoms on these shoots to perfume the room.

E. Satomi

A 400-year-old Japanese flowering apricot bonsai as it looks in winter.

This tree will grow in various soils and can stay in the same soil in the container for years.

In the growing season, particularly in the early half, liquid fertilizer should be applied several times. In the resting period, rape cake or soy bean cake should be placed on the soil. The container should be kept on the dry side until the flower buds for the next year are visible.

As we are bonsaimen, we have met many foreigners interested in bonsai at our Shubo-en bonsai-growing and sales yard in Tokyo. We hope the brief descriptions given here will give some helpful hints to friends in other countries who may wish to grow dwarfed potted trees, or bonsai.

23

HOW TO REPOT BONSAI

Root pruning is a key-technique

Yuji Yoshimura

Why is it necessary to change soil and cut roots?

There are two reasons: 1. The root systems of dwarfed potted trees get pot-bound just like any other plants growing in pots. Repotting improves root aeration and drainage, and provides new soil into which the fine new absorbing roots can grow. 2. The other reason is to encourage the growth of fine roots by cutting off some of the larger roots. From the cut ends ("stumps") of the larger roots, many fine roots will grow. This procedure keeps the bonsai root system always young.

How often should bonsai be repotted?

Roughly speaking, deciduous trees should be repotted once in two or three years; evergreen conifers, once in three to five years. If the roots grow very rapidly, like willow or crape-myrtle, they need an additional repotting at the end of each summer.

If the tree is not "pot bound," repotting can be delayed. For example, if there is as much as 1 or 2 inches of soil around the rim of the container that is not filled with roots, then repotting can be delayed one to two years longer.

For a tree in an 8- to 10-inch container, after repotting there should be about 2 inches of new soil between the root mass and the outer rim of the container. The new roots grow into this fresh soil.

If the tree is planted on a stone so the roots more or less clasp the stone, the stone and the roots are never separated from each other during repotting.

When is the best season to repot?

It is *best* to repot all kinds of bonsai in the early spring just as the new buds swell and start to grow, but before the leaves appear. Evergreen needle trees (conifers) also can be repotted just at the beginning of autumn, because they have a period of autumn rot growth. Deciduous trees can be repotted in late spring to summer, if it seems necessary. In this case, cut off all the larger leaves, letting only tiny new ones remain. If deciduous bonsai are repotted in late autumn or winter, they must be kept at spring temperatures after repotting.

If the repotting consists only of shifting the plant to another container, with little or no pruning of the root system, it can be done at any season.

After care

Repotting, with its accompanying drastic root pruning, is a shock to the tree which therefore needs special attention for three weeks or more after the repotting operation. Its after-care is similar, in a way, to that of a cutting—which must be kept in a humid atmosphere, with proper soil moisture, and protected from direct sun and wind. And it should not be out in heavy rain because the surface soil may wash away. However, in the case of early spring transplanting of deciduous bonsai

As much as one-half of the bottom roots are cut off flat before replanting the tree

24

Strands of copper wire are threaded through the drainage holes of the container, as shown in middle sketch, before the tree is replaced, as above. Upon finishing step "6" (*see text*), twist wire tight with pliers (lower right), so that roots are firmly held in position (lower left). This is step "7"

Eva Melady

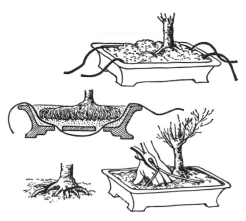

(before the buds burst), it is not necessary to protect the trees from direct sun. It is very important after repotting that all the soil, *including that close around the trunk*, be watered twice daily with a fine spray. Never fertilize until a month after repotting.

Usual method of repotting

Do not water bonsai just before repotting; it is difficult to remove the old soil if it is too wet. New soil must be dry and generally is a mixture of clay, peat moss, leaf mold and sand, in equal parts. Each of the soil components should be sifted in order to separate the different sized particles (see page 91, "The Care and Management of Bonsai").

The most necessary tools and materials are as follows:

Sharp scissors, a round brush (see illustration), pointed chopstick, wire clip-

pers, watering can (preferably one with fine spray), copper wire in a range of sizes, string, and dried and powdered moss which has grown on rock, i.e., a low growing moss.

The important ten steps:

1) Take tree out of container and clean out container with brush.

2) Prepare container. If the root mass of the bonsai will fill one-half to two-thirds of the space in the container after roots are trimmed, use copper wire to tie the tree in place. Arrange wire as illustrated, above; tie (later) as shown. If the

Sectional diagram through container showing method of holding a newly transplanted specimen tightly in position. Stick sharpened at one end and thrust through root ball.

Heavy cord, tied around the main stem several times above the container, and tightly drawn under the pot, will secure the plant and keep the main stem in desired position.

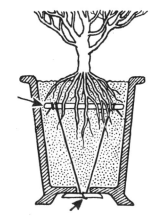

bamboo
stick

copper
wire

Frese

Buhle

Dry soil is firmed between tree roots with chopsticks, using a rapid up-and-down motion (step "6")

Surplus soil is brushed away to bring final level slightly lower than container rim (step "8")

root system is small, it is better to tie with string after the repotting is finished (see drawing page 25, lower right).

3) Loosen the soil of the root mass. Use chopstick to loosen up the outer one-third of the soil of the root mass. Also loosen soil of the underside of the root mass (approximately the lower third).

4) Trim roots. Use large sharp scissors and cut away the outer third of the fibrous mass; also cut off about half of the roots on the underside. A little tree should *not* be repotted if it does not have a tightly packed root system, that is, if it is not completely "pot bound."

5) Position tree in container. Place tree in center if the container is round or square, and one-third in from the end if a rectangular or oval container.

6) Get new soil in around the roots (see above). This is done by rapid jabbing with a chopstick. The soil *should not* be pressed down by hand. Only the chopstick can make the soil go into the spaces between the roots. The jabbing motion should not be to the same depth each time. That is to say, the first motion should go down deep, and the next time a little shallower than before, etc. Also jab sideways as well as straight down. Generally speaking, this jabbing motion takes time. For instance, it was necessary

to do it 15 minutes for the tree pictured at the left above. As the soil works down in and disappears, during the jabbing, constantly add more—until no more is needed.

7) Tie tree to container. Wires must be pulled up first then drawn together over the root mass, and twisted tight. There are several different ways of doing this (see drawings).

8) Brush away excess soil. If the surface soil is higher than the rim of the container, all the water will run off when the tree is sprinkled. Keep soil one-quarter inch lower than the side of the container. It is desirable to insert a protective rubber strip between wire and roots, so the wire will neither contact nor cut into the roots. Visible wire may be cut away after one growing season.

9) At this point only one finishing touch is needed. Spread a very thin layer of top soil over the surface of the soil already in the container, and sprinkle dried powdered moss, through the fingers, onto the top soil.

10) Water. Place the newly planted bonsai container in a tub of water in which the water level is the same depth as the container. At the same time, gently water from above.

FOR BONSAI BEGINNERS

The problems of wiring, watering and winter care, suggestions on containers.

Kan Yashiroda

Bonsai for Enduring Interest

I AM not a young man—59 years; I want to start with some interest that will hold throughout the rest of my life, and in my introduction to bonsai trees I feel sure I have found it.

When a Japanese speaks thus to other Japanese, he is very often told he is growing old, in a cynical tone—or is it an utterance of envy? Be it cynicism or envy or anything else, he is entering into a pleasant continual activity in growing and training bonsai, and at the same time doing something good for his health, to keep him mentally alert and physically sound. He is not entering upon the pursuit "simply to waste time."

The author of one of the articles in this issue (page 43) is an actor by profession, like the man who expressed the above conviction; similarly, too, he lives in a big city. If this man will follow the example of the Japanese actor, he can grow, train, and enjoy many miniature bonsai in his New York apartment, in his two very tiny glass houses, one holding twenty-four 2-inch pots and the other, thirty-eight. Mr. Nakamura grows all of his miniature bonsai on shelves on the roof of his house in Tokyo.

Again and again in Japan one comes across a moving van piled with goods and chattels and carrying on the top some bonsai, which are troublesome goods to move. In many cases those bonsai are not worth a dollar in money; but the owner will tell you that he has

The author, holding two miniature bonsai

cherished this one for the last fifteen years, that he collected that one on Mt. So-and-so and has kept it in the same container for thirty years, and so on. Enduring beauty and renewed interest in training and trimming those bonsai every year enchant him indefinitely.

Fifty-year-old Japanese beech (*Fagus cre-*
nata) growing over a stone, with roots
extending into the soil

E. Satomi photos

Trident maple (*Acer buergerianum*) with
its aged roots clasping a rock

75-year-old- azalea growing over a stone with roots extending into the soil container

Containers

What about selecting the proper containers, and should they have drainholes?

All containers have one or more drain holes; otherwise the trees will not be healthy but will look sickly and finally die.

On page 96 there are suggestions about choosing containers, and the Brooklyn Botanic Garden Women's Auxiliary offers many kinds (from Japan) for sale. As to drainholes and their importance:

A basin (for holding water) is a different thing, used for a different purpose. It is *never* used for growing bonsai directly. Sometimes grasses and rushes are grown on clumps of dead organic material in water-holding containers. If you have a tree that does well in soil saturated with moisture, such as bald cypress (page 58), you may place the container in which it is growing in a basin of water. Bonsai trees growing on stones are sometimes put into basins of water; but many such trees have their roots spread into soil in the containers, as shown on the opposite page; these containers are the regular ones with drain holes.

180-year-old flowering apricot (*Prunus mume*). This venerable bonsai spent its first 120 years in a garden and is now in its 60th year in a container.

What proportion between tree and container do you advise?

What is generally considered the ideal or artistic proportion is the tree 80 per cent and the container 20 per cent; or for dwarfer shrubs or low spreading trees, the plant 60 per cent and the container 40 per cent. In general, the smaller containers are better.

In a shallow oblong or elliptical container, the tree should be planted at a point 70 per cent of the distance from the right or the left end, according to the spread and shape of the branches, as shown on the preceding page. In a square or round container, the plant is placed in the center, except cascade forms; these are planted toward the edge, as illustrated on page 32.

E. Satomi

Flowering apricot. When containers are square or round, the trees are placed approximately in the center.

Pruning

I need information on pruning, both theory and practice.

Both root pruning and proper pruning of branches are important elements in dwarfing bonsai. The constant renewal or re-growth of the root system is essential to the proper health of the trunk and branches above ground. The root system will itself remain healthy only if properly pruned. This operation is associated with transplanting, and detailed directions will be found on pages 24 and 94. The fundamental virtue in root pruning is to keep the root system "happily" within the limited dimensions of a container.

There are two basic reasons for pruning the branches of bonsai. Many species that make splendid bonsai would grow into huge trees if not constantly pruned. It is chiefly by proper pruning that the artistic shape of bonsai is achieved.

Cascade - style Japanese white pine (*Pinus parviflora*). Even in round containers, trees trained in this style are planted toward the edge.

I procured ten specimens of Colorado blue spruce *(Picea pungens glauca)* **two years old, which had been transplanted twice. They were about 8 to 10 inches tall, with a good root structure. I obtained them in the fall and put them into 4-inch pots, but none of them survived the winter. What was the cause of the failure?**

I think you pruned off many roots in order to plant the trees in 4-inch pots, and there was not enough time for the formation of new rootlets before winter came.

If you cannot wait until spring, prune lightly and pot early in the fall to give ample time for new root formation.

Still better, plant in slightly larger pots than the ones in which you desire to grow and train the trees; the following spring or early fall, prune the roots and shift into the smaller pots.

It is a general rule that whenever ordinary nursery-grown stocks are intended for bonsai, they are first kept in a specially prepared bed for a few years. Bending and shaping may be started while plants are in such a bed, using copper wire as illustrated on page 65. They then are shifted into containers, larger ones at first, smaller ones finally.

Another way is to plant nursery-grown trees in larger pots than one thinks necessary, and gradually shift them into smaller and smaller ones over a period of several years.

Thirty-year-old Japanese white pine planted in center of round container

E. Satomi

Suppose I find a tree 3 feet tall at a commercial nursery that has healthy low-growing limbs and other qualities that would make a good bonsai. Shall I buy it?

Yes. But understand that it will need special culture. When you get home with it (assuming that it was balled and burlapped at the nursery), here are the main steps to take: 1) Pot it in a container large enough not to disturb the root ball. This may be a large commercial clay pot or a small wooden tub. Better yet, make a square or rectangular container, 6 to 8 inches high and just wide enough to accommodate the root ball. Fill in with additional soil around the root ball, and press firmly. Leave an inch at the top of

the container to facilitate adequate watering. 2) A tree 3 feet high is too tall for a good bonsai. Cut off the terminal 1½ feet (approximately). Make the cut just above a side branch that can then be wired into the terminal position. Trim the new terminal branch as seems indicated, also the side branches. 3) After 2 years in the container, with appropriate and continuous pruning and wiring of side branches, as needed, the tree should be transplanted to a container of smaller dimensions, both shallower and smaller in diameter.

After a year or two in the smaller container, transplant to a still smaller authentic bonsai pot, and you are on your way!

Certain varieties of Japanese maple have small leaves which makes them especially desirable as bonsai. This specimen is 80 years old.

E. Satomi

Leaves Out of Proportion

Is there any way to avoid having the leaves out of proportion with the size of the dwarfed tree?

Reduction in size of leaves does not usually parallel the degree of the dwarfing of the tree: in the course of dwarfing, the leaves show little evidence of becoming smaller.

We select smaller-leaved varieties or clones for bonsai in the first place. Many trees used as bonsai have shorter- or smaller-leaved varieties or clones in one district or another; this is true of Japanese zelkova (*Z. serrata*), beeches (*Fagus*), elms (*Ulmus*), Japanese white and black pines (*Pinus parviflora* and *thunbergi*), Sargent juniper (*Juniperus chinensis sargenti*), Yeddo spruce (*Picea jezoensis*), and many other trees.

One may think that such a problem does not concern needle-leaved trees; but Japanese bonsai fanciers recognize several clones or strains of the trees mentioned above, and are careful to secure their material from the particular district in which the desired clone or strain grows naturally. I cannot describe the distinctions scientifically, but I can clearly identify the different clones or strains at a glance.

In American trees, also, a keen observer with artistic taste in color and form may find some clone or strain which botanists do not consider worth separating but which is more suitable for bonsai. The distinction may be a minor one; but when these trees are grown as bonsai, *it is the minor distinction that makes one tree predominate over its fellows.*

Trees that have been cultivated for centuries have many varieties and forms, and generally some of these are smaller-leaved or dwarfed in nature. Many varieties will to some extent do away with the complaint of the disproportionately large size of the leaves when the trees are dwarfed. Such varieties exist particularly in Japanese maples (*Acer*), heavenly-bamboo (*Nandina domestica*), pomegranate (*Punica granatum*), magnolias, camellias (*C. japonica* and *C. sasanqua*), Kurume and Satsuki azaleas (*Rhododendron obtusum amoenum* and *R. indicum*), Japanese flowering apricot (*Prunus mume*), and flowering quinces (*Chaenomeles*).

In certain kinds of broad-leaved trees, sometimes all the leaves are pinched off when they are practically mature. This causes new leaves to be formed which are smaller and which will be brighter in autumn color in such trees as trident maple (*Acer buergerianum*) and other maples.

In other cases, the growing branches are cut back to dormant buds to induce these to become active and the resultant leaves may be smaller. The new sprouts are regulated by pinching the strongest ones off entirely by reducing them to one or two leaves; then a third sprouting, with smaller leaves, may be expected from the axillary buds or dormant buds.

The leaves of bonsai are healthier, brighter, and neater in appearance when the plants are kept in a sunny site, are not allowed to become water-logged, and are properly fertilized. It would not be a good idea to give no fertilizer at all or to use a fertilizer without nitrogen.

When the size of the leaves is incommensurate with the size of the tree from an æsthetic point of view, thinning of leaves is practiced; this relieves the feeling of disproportionateness to some extent.

Whenever large broad-leaved trees are trained as bonsai, the branches are greatly reduced; with a few branches the bonsai is formed into an artistic shape and the place each leaf fills is carefully considered. In other words, when the leaves are fully expanded, each leaf takes the place of a branch from the æsthetic point of view; and so the leaves do not seem so greatly out of proportion.

In Japan one often sees pine needles cut in half to remedy an untidy appearance, but this does not look so nice, and I have never wished to try it, myself.

Thinning the needles, taking off the older ones on each shoot to relieve the heavy feeling, and shortening the needles by cutting off the upper half or so, are general practices with pines in Japanese gardens and as bonsai.

Kurume azalea (*Rhododendron obtusum amoenum*), with small leaves and small flowers

Water

Should one deprive the little trees of as much water as possible?

Bonsai should be kept drier than ordinary ornamental plants in pots; but if the object is to dwarf the trees or to keep them dwarfed, it is no use to make them bone-dry. Want of water only makes them stunted or unhealthy.

If there is such a thing as a fundamental principle in watering bonsai, it is this: water liberally but be sure that the soil drains amply. In most cases, it does not matter how many times a day bonsai are watered if the soil has perfect drainage and does not hold the slightest excess of water. This explains why many bonsai growers are kept busy with watering, particularly in hot dry weather; and why bonsai kept outdoors are never water-logged even in the rainy season in Japan, though the rain pours down day after day.

This fundamental principle may be modified to suit the individual case, according to the kind of soil obtainable, the climate, the kinds of trees grown, the containers used, and the amount of time one can spare each day for bonsai.

Black and red pines trained as bonsai in the districts around the Seto Inland Sea, where the climate is sunny and dry, generally become longer-needled when brought to Tokyo or thereabouts; the reason is that it is less sunny and the air contains more moisture.

I once told a New Yorker: "If New York's air is saturated with spirits (as an American lady in Italy said) or saturated with any other moisture, you must always keep your containers drier than usual. If you keep them on the wet side, the leaves will be in hopeless condition—large, thin, and untidy."

The New Yorker has corrected my view by saying: "The only thing that saturates this city's air is dirt and soot." Dirt and soot are also troublesome and dangerous to bonsai. Unless the leaves are always kept clean, the branches become weak; gradually the smaller and weaker ones die, leaving only the upper, stronger ones and the bonsai become spindling and unsightly.

Louis Buhle

A Japanese white pine bonsai on which the training wires have been painted white to make them show in the photograph

A 10-year-old Yeddo spruce (*Picea jezoensis*) showing how the wires are placed for training

Wiring
How is the tree trained with wire?

The accompanying photograph shows the way better than I can describe it.

The amount of water given daily should be reduced for two or three days before the operation takes place; this puts the tree into better condition for the wiring by making it somewhat limp and pliable.

Copper wire is prepared for use by being burned in a fire. In Japan a rice-straw fire is always used because it does not become too hot; wire thus annealed and slowly cooled is easy to bend. However, once bent, it hardens in a short time, thus holding a bonsai trunk or branch firmly in place. If the wire is burned too long in a fire that is too hot, it becomes dry, brittle, and difficult to coil. If the wire is heated in a gas flame, it should be brought only to red heat—then allowed to cool.

One end of the burned copper wire is inserted deep into the soil near the base of the trunk to be trained. It is then coiled upward but not in firm contact with the trunk or branches. To avoid damaging the bark or leaving the marks of the wire on it, the trunk is often covered with hemp bark before the wire is coiled. The bark of a cryptomeria tree, rice straw, pieces of split bamboo, and the like may be used in place of hemp bark. For delicate and soft-barked trees and shrubs such as azaleas, the wire is covered with cloth, paper, or the like, before it is used.

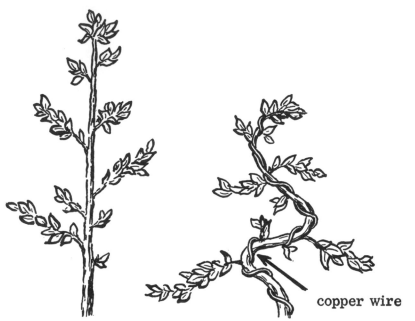

copper wire

Left, an upright azalea. *Right,* the same azalea bent into a curve and held in position with copper training wire.

The photograph on the previous page shows a 10-year-old Yeddo spruce (*Picea jezoensis*); just before the buds opened, the branches were thinned and the trunk and branches were trained with wires.

When the coiling is finished, the bending begins. Holding the base of the trunk in the left hand and the upper end of the wire in the right, bend the trunk into approximately the desired position. Then make the more minute and delicate bends, one by one. The training of the branches follows.

This technique is suitable for slender trunks and small branches. With stouter trunks, bending must precede wire coiling.

One could easily take the upper half of the trunk of the tree in the photograph, and bend it horizontally in a moment. The principle of wire-coiling, however, is that after the trunk is bent into the desired shape with the hands—very cautiously and patiently—wire coiling follows to fix the trunk in that shape.

Whenever the trunk has once been bent, it *must not* be restored to its former position but must be held in the bent position until the wire coiling is finished to fix it that way. If a thick trunk or branch is bent sharply, the soft inner tissues on the outer (or convex) side of the curve are greatly damaged; but similar tissues on the inner (or concave) side of the curve are uninjured and continue to function and promote the healing of the damaged part. However, if the trunk is restored to its former position after it is once bent, all the inner tissues are likely to be damaged so that the tree will die.

Let me repeat: before bending or wiring, the trunk or branch should be protected with hemp-palm rope, manila rope, cloth, bark, or the like; paper will do for very slender branches.

For a very thick trunk, which cannot be trained with wires, the expert uses a vise; but that is not good for the tree.

An azalea grown upright in a nursery

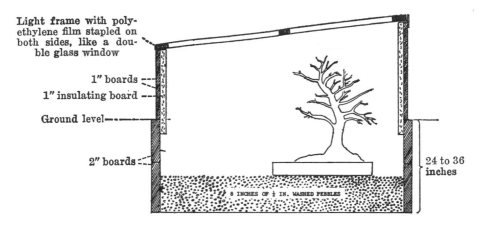

Sectional view of deep coldframe suitable for the winter storage of bonsai in cold climates. The frame should be situated in shaded area completely free of winter sun (lath house shade is satisfactory). Plastic covered sash on top should fit tightly. As many as 30 plants can be stored in a 5- by 6-foot frame.

row, like the one in the sketch, or any azalea with its branches thinned till it looked like this, could easily be trained into the curve shown in the sketch in an hour or two. Azaleas grown in greenhouses are better for training.

Winter Care

What do I need to know about winter care?

Winter care differs for hardy and nonhardy or tender plants.

Hardy plants are those that can live outdoors in the coldest weather without danger of winterkilling. They are *not* house plants but are real outdoor plants. Typical examples are many kinds of pine, spruce, yew, retinospora (*Chamaecyparis* species), hemlock, cedar, larch, holly, maple, privet, flowering crab-apple, hawthorn, rockspray, etc. These plants need winter cold to remain healthy and grow well. But be cautious!

Hardy species growing in bonsai containers present a special problem if left outdoors in below-freezing winter weather. Soil in the containers will freeze, and the containers will break. Moreover, it is impossible to properly water bonsai growing in firmly frozen soil.

If a sunporch or cold but light room is available where the night temperature never falls below about 36°F., this would provide a good place for overwintering hardy or semi-hardy bonsai.

Here is another suggestion for overwintering hardy or semi-hardy bonsai in a freezing climate: keep them in an insulated deep cold-frame. It should be shaded by a lath house. The soil in bonsai pots, with such protection, should never freeze if the night temperatures do not go much below 0° F. The bonsai should be watered as needed, and on warmer non-freezing winter days, it is well to remove the protective covering and give the plants full air. Be sure to replace the covering sash before sunset!

Many non-hardy or tender species trained as bonsai will grow satisfactorily if treated as house plants. In a loose sense they might even be called "house plant" bonsai. Typical plants in this group would include tender azalea, camellia, gardenia, bix, dwarf pomegranate, firethorn, rosemary, and any other tender species with small leaves, flowers and fruit that might lend themselves well to bonsai training.

Kinds of Plants

What kinds of small trees or shrubs might I buy at a nursery that could be grown in pots and trained as bonsai?

Accompanying articles help answer this question; also see inside back cover.

It is not necessary to have the dense, symmetrically branched young trees which are nice for foundation planting. Young trees irregularly branched but not stunted, having a broadly pyramidal outline, generally suit the purpose well enough. In other words, it is preferable to have a very stout or the stoutest branch at the base, and one nearly as stout, or equally so next above the base. If the lowest branches are not the stout-

est, they will become weakened in the course of years of dwarfing and will eventually be in very poor condition or die. Thus the tree will lose its good proportions and æsthetic shape and become top-heavy and spindling.

Opposite branching is avoided in bonsai. However, when young trees are selected for training, it is not necessary to avoid the opposite-branched ones; these can be changed into alternate-branched trees by cutting off one of the two opposite branches.

In the nursery rows, one should select young trees that have been well transplanted and root-pruned, especially those with spreading shallow roots, which are better suited to shallow containers. Trees

The spirit of bonsai is well portrayed by this Japanese maple (*Acer palmatum*). An ancient tree growing in nature would have the same gnarled limbs and roots left bare by soil erosion.

E. Satomi

Gray-barked elm, or
Japanese zelkova
(*Z. serrata*)

E. Satomi

having some stout roots near the surface of the soil are easier to keep dwarf and healthy. The roots and rootlets in the lower part of the container can easily be renewed; and bonsai of certain trees, such as maples (*Acer*) and Japanese zelkova (*Z. serrata*), feature roots on the surface of the soil, as shown here.

For making a miniature forest from one tree, as shown on pages 2, 17, and 74, avoid a young tree with stout lower branches and choose one with branches as nearly as posible equal in vigor and length. The latter is more likely to produce uniform growth of the branches which are eventually to look like independent trees.

Aside from restraining the roots in a small container, what you advise for dwarf Canary Island date palms (*Phoenix canariensis*)?

I am growing in my Acclimatization Garden, some tall trees of palms—date palm (*Phoenix*), coconut (*Cocos*), Washington palm (*Washingtonia*), palmetto (*Sabal*), and some others. From seeds which have fallen from these palms, seedlings are growing naturally and abundantly, thousands of them close together. Seedlings growing thus show very little development, except those at the margin of the colony; yet I have never seen any dwarfed one worth cultivating.

California redwood (*Sequoia sempervirens*). It was a spindly rooted cutting 12 years before this picture was taken.

Are any of the truly "great-trees" suitable for bonsai?

Yes, California redwood, whose Latin name *sempervirens* means "constant life," can be trained as a bonsai. The fact that it may grow several hundred feet tall and is known to have lived more than 3,000 years in its native California mountains and valleys does not mean that it can't be kept small by systematic pruning of roots and shoots. The photograph above shows how redwood can be trained in perfect harmony with its container. The spaces between branches are just as important as the masses of foliage. The needles live 3 or 4 years and do not drop individually, as in most evergreens, but fall with the spray-like clusters. Constant pruning by working the branches back toward the center of the tree is important if redwood is to be successfully grown as a bonsai.

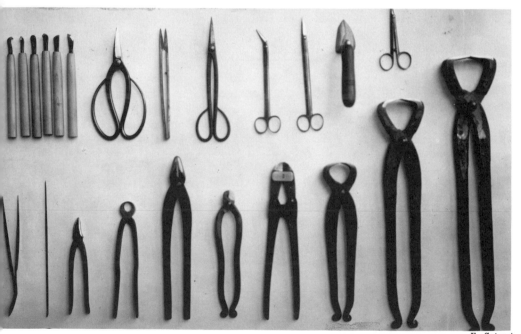

E. Satomi

Tools used in bonsai culture includes small special knives, various scissors, pincers, and Clippers

Mr. Nakamura and part of his collection of bonsai and some of the tiny containers in which he grows them.

MINIATURE BONSAI

How to raise and enjoy them

Zeko Nakamura*

F OR the past twenty years I have been growing and enjoying miniature dwarfed potted plants, or *Mame bonsai*, as a hobby. I have endeavored to create ever smaller miniature bonsai, in smaller pots than have ever been used before. Indeed, I am growing these plants with the minimum amount of soil in the smallest pots in which they can live.

Water. The main point is that they are given plenty of water: in the summer they are watered about five or six

---

*The writer's name is well known among Japanese as a comedian on stage and screen, but his hobby of miniature, or *Mame*, bonsai is known only among professional and amateur fanciers of bonsai. Having no garden space, he is growing all his hundreds of miniature bonsai on the roof, as is often done in a big city like Tokyo. While he was a young priest in southern Japan, where he was born, he was interested in growing the plants found on the mountains and in the fields around the temple. That interest was intensified on his return to secular life and grew to the maximum when he went to live in the big city. This is the first time he has ever taken his pen in hand to write on the growing and training of Mame bonsai (pronounced *mah-may bone-sigh*)—Guest Ed.

times a day; and even in the winter, they must be watered once a day by all means.

Soil. Since a great deal of water is applied, it is essential that the soil be well drained. Fine copper wire netting is placed over the hole in the bottom of the pot, for perfect drainage; this is covered by a layer of soil with particles the size of grains of rice; finally the pot is filled with soil having finer particles (the size of grains of millet). Both of these soils consist of a mixture of equal amounts of red clay subsoil and fertilized topsoil. These well sieved granulated soils allow good drainage and never hold excessive water. Even when water is given every thirty minutes, it runs through the hole immediately, and so the soil is kept sweet and well aerated. The soil may be sterilized before use, to destroy insects and disease-producing organisms. When I bring soil home, I sieve it into three or four grades according to sizes of particles and expose it to the sun for several days until it is smooth and dry as sand.

43

Some of the writer's miniature bonsai brought indoors and arrange

Potting. Before putting the plant into the pot, the root system should be examined and the older roots removed. One should then see which side of the plant is best to face the spectator. If a rectangular or elliptical container is used, the tree should be planted toward one end, the right or left end according to the shape of the tree; in either case it should be placed at a point seven-tenths of the distance from one end and just back of the middle. That is the best spot, not only from an aesthetic point of view, but for trimming, training, and developing the plant.

The plant should be watered as soon as it is potted. For a week or so, the pot should be kept in half-shade and the foliage sprayed freely; then it should be placed in the sun half of the day for four or five days, and after that, exposed to the sun all day.

Fertilizer. I make my own fertilizer, of dried fish. I pulverize the fish, add water, and keep it in a covered jar for half a year or a year or more. Then I use the clear liquid in the upper part of the jar, diluting it fifty to 100 times.

Rape cake, soy bean cake, and herring cake are equally good.† Fertilizer should be applied to miniature bonsai generally once a week. (Also see page 95.)

As Mame bonsai are wee lovely things, often displayed in the living room and admired in the palm of the hand, these fertilizers should not be placed on the surface of the soil but should be applied only in liquid form. The liquid fertilizer is made as just described and diluted as mentioned or diluted until the liquid is without smell or only very slightly odorous.

Containers. By comparison with the ordinary, larger bonsai, Mame bonsai are lacking in grand appearance; and so

George Kalmbacher

---

†These fertilizers have been sold for centuries in Japan and are extensively used. Comparable plant foods here are fish emulsion fertilizer and cottonseed meal. (See p. 95—Ed.)

Pyracantha bonsai

...or display. Cigarette packages among plants give an idea of their size.

I train them to look like the larger bonsai or like the mature big trees. Also I prefer to use pretty pots or pans or containers, as this ornamental earthenware is in itself greatly to be admired. In the prewar days, I used to make and bake the containers at the pottery; but those and other containers, as well as all of my plants, were turned into ashes when my house was burned by a bombing during the war. My present collection of Mame bonsai and containers, as seen in the accompanying photographs, has been made and grown since peace has come to us.

Length of life. Unless one is careless, miniature bonsai will not die; they may live through three generations of man— grandfather, father, and son. Some trees which are 1¼ inches tall when full-grown will live through several decades if well cared for. In my twenty years of growing several hundred of these tiny trees, I do not remember that one has died because of any fault in watering, fertilizing, or other care. I am always amazed to hear of the death of such plants.

General care. Since Mame bonsai are very little things, some fanciers say that it is better to grow them indoors or under bamboo blinds or in half-shade or in a cold frame, but I think it is better to grow them in full sunlight and exposed to all changes of season.

Except when I am afraid they might be blown away by strong winds, I keep them outdoors on the growing shelf all the time, even in the cold season. However, in Tokyo, if the plants remain outdoors in January, February, and March, the containers are often broken by freezing; and so they are brought indoors for these three months.

Some Mame bonsai, growing in larger containers, pass the whole winter outdoors without having their containers broken, though they are occasionally covered with snow and severe frosts are experienced every day. In such cases the growth in the spring is finer.

Cotoneaster microphylla bonsai.

45

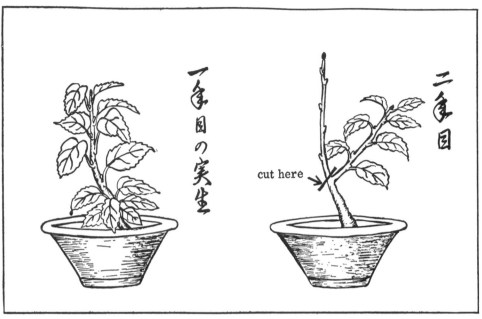

一年目の実生　　　二年目

cut here

Adapted from author's diagrams

One-year-old seedling, ready for pruning to shape its trunk

Two-year-old seedling. Note upright shoot removed, lateral branch allowed to grow

On windy days and on hot summer days, when the moisture is quickly dried out of the tiny containers, ice is given liberally. On some summer days when I was on the stage of a theater in the center of Tokyo, I took advantage of an hour and a half between two of my acts and went home, 3½ miles away, to give ice to each of my little plants. Now, when I am often away from home for months, my mother, wife, and children take care of my plants with interest and pleasure; and so I have no fear of losing any of my Mame bonsai.

Subjective value. Next to motion pictures and plays, with which I am professionally concerned, I seem to be living for Mame bonsai. Whenever I am at leisure here and there in Japan, I search for naturally dwarfed small things suitable for this kind of culture. I bring them home, plant them in containers, and grow and train them as nice Mame bonsai. Raising miniatures from such natural material, or from seeds I sow myself, or from material obtained by air-layering bigger trees, is far more satisfying than spending money for materials or purchasing Mame bonsai to admire.

It takes five to ten years to produce a Mame bonsai worthy of the name or fit to be admired. Indeed, it is a trial of patience between man and tree. It seems to me that this pursuit is good for hasty men in big cities in this hurried age; I feel that such impatient men learn to be deliberate as they become interested in raising Mame bonsai. In the course of growing and training these miniatures for years, a great deal of pleasure and satisfaction should be experienced.

Training

Now let me tell you the way to trim and train Mame bonsai.

Like nature. The best style for them is to follow the nature of the materials used. They should be miniatures of Nature's giants. A miniature bonsai of a large-growing tree is trimmed like the

46

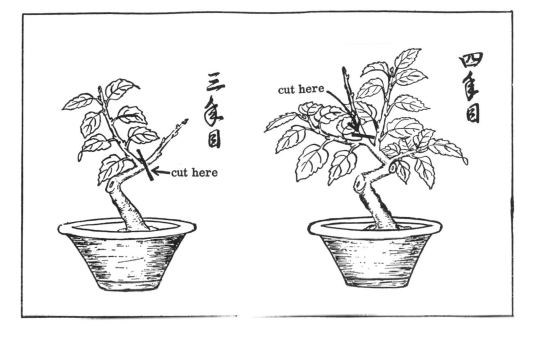

| Three-year-old tree, showing further training by pruning | Four-year-old tree: trunk beginning to assume picturesque form |

mature shape of that kind of tree, though of course it is for smaller in size. Mame bonsai shrubs are like mature shrubs in shape and style; and Mame bonsai herbaceous plants are like herbaceous clumps in miniature. Thus, Japanese zelkova is broom-shape, cryptomeria is columnar, and pines are in the shapes characteristic of old specimens.

If the habitat of a certain tree is to have a straight vertical trunk, the material selected for Mame bonsai of this tree should be young straight-growing ones. If another has, in nature, thick roots spreading in all directions on the ground, the young tree selected should have its taproot cut off short so that it will have good development of roots on the surface in the future.

Wiring and pruning. The trunk is trained with copper wire which has been previously burned in the fire to make it more easily managed. However, it is imposible to train young trees 1 to 2 inches tall with copper wire at an early age. Therefore a 1- or 2-year-old tree should be cut off at a dormant bud ⅜ to ¾ inch from the base; after one or two years more it should be cut off an inch or so from the base. After such cutting back has been repeated for four or five years, the trunk gradually becomes interesting, looking like an old dwarfed one. Some tiny branches are formed very low; the lowest one should be kept longest and the uppermost, shortest; they are pinched back with the finger nail while they are very young. The manner of cutting back the leader to form a very dwarfed and interestingly shaped trunk is shown in the accompanying sketches.

In contrast with the one illustrated here, cryptomeria is straight-trunked in nature and shows its maximum beauty in that form. The trunk of cryptomeria is repeatedly cut back year after year, to make it shorter and thicker, to have branches as low as possible, and to keep them healthy. If the trunk becomes bent

47

Young cryptomeria, showing where the leader is to be cut to keep tree dwarfed.

can readers, or those in other parts of the world, may well be amused at the idea of annealing heavy copper wire in a rice straw fire (so it will bend easily). Most kinds of straw should be equally satisfactory, the only point being that the flame should not be too hot.

Cryptomeria japonica is one of the most valued timber conifers in Japan. Two specimens are shown in the accompanying photograph. The smaller one is only 1¾ inches tall, while the other is 14⅜ inches tall. The smaller one is the parent tree, 10 years old, from one of whose branches the bigger one was raised as a cutting taken two years ago and potted last year. Next year, in the spring, this young tree will be cut off about 1⅛ to 1¼ inches from the base; it will be gradually dwarfed, being placed in smaller containers year after year until it becomes a Mame bonsai. In the course of dwarfing, particularly, and also afterward, the growing tips of young shoots should be pinched off as regular pruning procedure.

or twisted, copper wire should be coiled spirally around it from the base up, as shown in the sketch. The trunk can then be straightened, and the wire kept on until the trunk is fixed in the right shape and position. Copper wire burned in a fire of rice straw is most easily managed and best to use for training. Ameri-

A second cut has been made, on the new leader, and a third leader is developing. This procedure, repeated year after year, keeps the tree dwarf.

Adapted from author's sketches

New leader developing from small branch just below first cut.

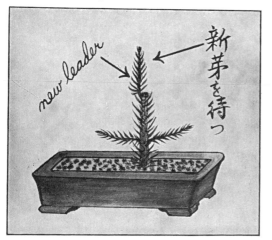

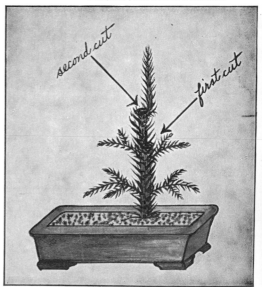

Drooping forms. If one wishes to have a Mame bonsai tree with drooping branches like those of old trees, it may be done by coiling copper wire around the branches and bending them downward, as is done with ordinary bonsai. However, since Mame bonsai are tiny things, the wires may cause damage; and so I sometimes hang a weight on the branch. to lower it.

The following is the way I usually do it and is the best way. The container is bound with string, somewhat as in tying a parcel, as shown in the sketch on the next page. The branches are lowered and held in the desired position by means of strings tied to them and fastened to the string around the con-

A small cryptomeria (*C. japonica*), 10 years old; and a 2-year-old tree raised from a cutting from the small one.

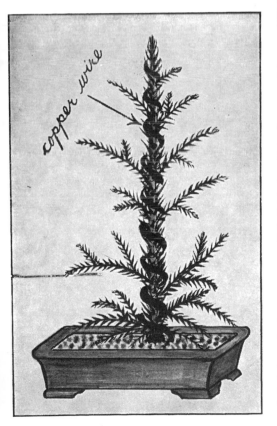

Young cryptomeria bonsai, wired to keep its trunk straight.

tainer. The strings are left on for several months, until the branches are fixed in the desired position.

Flowers and fruits. The shoots of flowering trees and shrubs should be pinched about the middle of June. (That is the beginning of the rainy season in Japan, and the young shoots are hardening.) Only about two buds should be left on each shoot; from these buds new branches will grow in July and August. These branches are to remain untouched until autumn; in November they should be shortened, leaving some flower buds which have formed. It is desirable to use a small pair of sharp pruning shears.

I do not take special care to induce my plants to form flower buds, but these develop well when the plants are exposed directly to the sun all the season, even on the hottest summer days.

As shown in the accompanying photographs, the containers for Mame bonsai are very small; one of the smallest is only ⅜ inch deep. Since the roots have

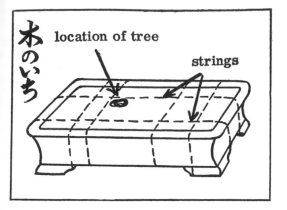

木のいち

location of tree

strings

Tray showing the proper position of placing the plant, and strings to which branches may be tied.

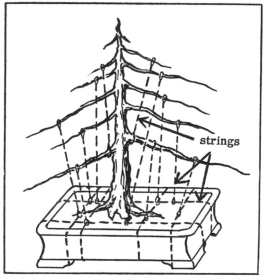

strings

A tree properly placed in the tray, with its branches tied to the strings around the container to pull them down into a drooping position.

so small a space in which to live and spread, in half a year (to say nothing of a year) they become bound in the container and often lift the soil some ¾ inch above the rim of the container.

Although they are very tiny in size, after becoming root-bound the flowering trees and shrubs produce flower buds in the normal season for each kind of plant. When the flower buds are formed, fer-

tilizing should be stopped. A fruit tree that has borne fruit should be given diluted liquid fertilizer again about two months after the flowers are shed; this fertilizing should be continued, with some intervals, until autumn.

My Mame bonsai flowering cherries and flowering apricots are only a few inches high, but they bloom well annually, while apple, crab apple, and pomegranate bear fruit. I have flowering and fruiting peaches, too. I deeply regret that the season is so far advanced that I am unable to show you these in flower and in fruit.

All the plants I am growing have small and neat leaves, as these are most suitable for Mame bonsai. Floribunda and Multiflora roses are blooming continuously and attain a height of 2 inches or so as Mame bonsai.

Repotting. To bear fruit, apple and crab apple trees should be repotted in the autumn, not in the spring. All fruit trees are repotted every autumn.

All the other trees and shrubs are repotted annually in the spring, say early April in Tokyo—except pines; these are repotted once in five or more years. Pine trees grow better if they are repotted once in three or four years, but then they grow too vigorously, break the balance of the trained branches, and cause some of the lesser ones to become weak and die.

The plant is taken out of the container and a large amount of soil is removed, very carefully, little by little, so as not to damage the roots. Then some of the older roots are cut off or shortened, and the other roots and rootlets are shortened slightly. The plants are repotted in the same containers filled with fresh soil of the same kind. They are then watered liberally. For about ten days after repotting, the plants must have special care; the oftener they are syringed, the better.

Herbaceous plants are generally kept without repotting for five to ten years; in this way they look better and become daintier.

Three miniature bonsai. *Left to right,* Japanese red pine (*Pinus densiflora*), 5 years old, 2 inches tall; red sandalwood (*Adenanthera pavonina*), 10 years old, 2¾ inches tall; Japanese black pine (*Pinus thunbergi*), about 30 years old, 3⅓ inches tall. The three empty containers are each ⅜ inch high and ¾ inch in diameter.

Two pomegranate seedlings, one 9 years old, 4 inches tall; the other 5 years old, 2¾ inches tall, in fruit. Below, old Japanese porcelain containers.

The author, holding in his left hand a miniature Japanese white pine (*Pinus parviflora*) and several of the small containers.

51

Summing Up

These are the essential points in growing Mame bonsai.

It is most important to keep the container well supplied with water. Adequate fertilizer must be given. The plants must be well exposed to the sun. The growing shelf must be well ventilated.

When the new shoots begin to harden, they are cut back or pinched off, with two buds left at the base of each. Strong water sprouts are never allowed to grow.

The plants should be trained in their natural shapes. It is better to train and trim with pruning shears than with wire.

Repotting at the proper time should never be neglected. As the plants are grown in very small containers, it is essential to cut off the older roots and encourage new ones to grow. The soil must be well drained. The plants must be kept particularly well watered for about ten days after repotting.

Soils are so varied in different places that I have not written in detail on soil. I am using many kinds of soil whenever they are available. Some trees need a particular kind of soil or compost, to be healthy in small containers; but each grower will soon find these.

In Japan the changes of the four seasons are clearly seen and felt. Flowers in the spring, dark green foliage in the summer, picturesque colors in the autumn—crimson, yellow, and other exquisite colors—and the still figures of deciduous trees in solitude in the winter, are all in poetic mood in nature. Also, and indeed in the same degree, such changes are shown in Mame bonsai growing in 1-inch containers.

Whenever you think that some of your own native plants are suitable to grow as Mame bonsai, take home some little ones and try them. It is not necessary to start with or buy finished Mame bonsai. You may bring home a few shells from the beach, make a hole in the bottom of each for drainage, fill them with soil, plant some young trees or herbaceous plants, and see how they will behave and grow. I should like, myself, to try some American plants as Mame bonsai if I could afford to live in America.

Mr. Nakamura with his 81-year-old mother, his wife, and his children, holding specimens of miniature bonsai. When Mr. Nakamura's stage appearances take him away from home, sometimes for months at a time, members of his family take care of "these wee lovely things."

THE MATSUDAIRA COLLECTION OF MINIATURE BONSAI

Some choice dwarfed plants and notes on their culture

Akiko Matsudaira*

*Mrs. Matsudaira is deeply devoted to miniature bonsai. For many years she shared her husband's enthusiasm for these tiny beautiful things. Her illustrious husband was the late Count Y. Matsudaira, a pioneer fancier of miniature bonsai, who had built up a magnificent collection second to none.

There are many anecdotes about his enthusiastic behavior regarding these plants. Whenever he was on a trip, he used to carry some of his favorite bonsai with him in a basket specially designed and made for the purpose.—Guest Ed.

AFTER the great earthquake occurred in Tokyo and caused much disaster, in 1923, the city was barren and monotonous. It was then that my husband began to collect miniature, or *Mame*, bonsai. In the mountains and in other places he visited on his trips, he collected and purchased them as souvenirs. During the years when he was at the height of his zest for these plants, he grew seven or eight hundred of them.

Some of the miniature bonsai grown by the writer in her garden.

Bamboo stand special-
ly designed for dis-
playing miniature
bonsai. The plants,
raised by the author,
are: *top*, needle juni-
per (*Juniperus rigi-
da*), 30 years; *middle*,
barberry (*Berberis
sieboldi*), 25 years;
below, left to right:
Chiogenes japonica,
10 years; maple, 25
years; an alpine plant,
10 years.

Crabapple, 25 years,
with twenty fruits

Rosewood stand especially designed for holding miniature bonsai. The species displayed here are 6 to 20 years of age and include Japanese holly (*Ilex crenata*), Sargent juniper (*Juniperus chinensis sargenti*), crabapple (*Malus* sp.), graybarked elm (*Zelkova serrata*), and Japanese white pine (*Pinus parviflora*).

Mitsukoshi Exhibition

I was faced with his death ten years ago, and during the war many of the miniature bonsai were destroyed by the bombing. Some of them were carried away from Tokyo to the country, to escape the dangers of war; but these suffered because I was short of hands, and some of them died. About two hundred survived and were brought here to Atami. Some of these are shown in the photographs.

The years mentioned for the plants are not their actual ages but the number of years I have been growing them.

Culture

Just after the equinox (the middle of March) every year, all the Mame bonsai are repotted in new soil. Diluted liquid fertilizer made from well fermented rape cake is applied to them often in the spring and in the autumn. (Also see page 95.)

Although they are tiny plants growing in very small containers, they are kept outdoors and exposed all day long to the hot sun and wind and rain, just like ordinary bonsai. In hot dry summer weather, they are watered three or four times a day.

To prevent ants from reaching the plants, all the legs of the growing shelf stand in water to which a few drops of insecticide have been added.

BONSAI AT THE
BROOKLYN BOTANIC GARDEN

WITHIN recent years the Brooklyn Botanic Garden has become recognized as one of the leading American sources of information on bonsai culture. The Garden has twice, in the last few years, brought bonsai experts from Japan not only to improve the quality of plants in the Garden's collection, but also to offer advanced courses in bonsai to all who might be interested. From one to two hundred people have taken such courses each year.

Friends of the Botanic Garden have made it possible to import many fine bonsai from Japan. In addition, our Japanese garden caretaker-gardener has trained additional plants from seedlings, cuttings and small nursery stock. Our collection has thus increased in size, and in addition a great many species and varieties have been tested to determine their suitability for bonsai.

In order to measure the expanding popular interest in bonsai culture, the Garden has from year to year staged small public exhibitions of bonsai, grown by amateur enthusiasts. This project has been linked to an annual plant sale sponsored by the Women's Auxiliary for the benefit of the Botanic Garden. Hundreds of visitors come to see the plants and to purchase surplus bonsai specimens, authentic imported containers, and accessories.

Buhle

(Left)

Japanese white pine in Brooklyn Botanic Garden collection. Gift of Mr. and Mrs. Howard Phipps

Pulitzer

(Right)

Pinus rigida, collected from wild. For better viewing side, see page 85.

Small-fruited crabapple in early autumn. Gift of Mr. and Mrs. Edward Holsten to the Botanic Garden collection

Same tree in winter, two years earlier, showing the branches trained in position by wiring

Maple "forest" in winter (trident maple, *Acer buergerianum*). Gift of Mr. and Mrs. Howard Phipps to the Botanic Garden collection

57

BALD CYPRESS BONSAI

From cuttings or from seedlings

Toyotaro Aoshima

BALD CYPRESS (*Taxodium disti-chum*) is a deciduous tree inhabiting swamps along the larger rivers in the southern part of the United States. It was introduced into Japan in the last century, and now many fine old trees are found here and there all over Japan.

A few decades ago, some bonsai fanciers were attracted by the graceful feathery, pleasing green foliage, slightly pendulous spreading branches, and massive trunk with cinnamon-brown bark. They set out to grow and train these trees as bonsai and the results were very successful. Bald cypresses are now highly thought of as bonsai, and a few of the oldest and best ones have been sold at high prices in the past year. As this tree is easy to train with copper wire, it should be tried by amateur as well as professional bonsai growers.

Bald cypress is called *Rakuusho,* or Feather-Falling-Pine in Japan, but bonsaimen prefer to call it Robe-of-Feather-Pine.

An acquaintance in an adjacent city had a very fine and well-trained bald cypress bonsai. I visited him, to take a photograph of the tree for this article, but it had been sold to a professional bonsai-man only the day before. Consequently all I can do is show one of my own comparatively young specimens. My tree is not a good example but it gives a vague idea how bald cypress is trained into bonsai to have a pleasing appearance. This tree was started by obtaining a very young tree raised from a cutting about ten years ago.

Cuttings are taken from the last year's growth; after the ends are cut cleanly with a sharp knife, the cuttings are inserted in clean sand kept moist. For the first two years the cuttings should be allowed to grow naturally, as in ordinary nursery stock.

Training. About the third year or so, one should begin to train them with copper wire, bending the trunk and branches as one likes. Before training is begun, the longer branches should be cut

Bald cypress bonsai about 12 years old grown by the writer

Bald cypress growing in its native habitat in southern United States, showing the buttressed trunks and the projecting root branches called "knees"

Avery

Bald cypress about 60 years old, showing the slender pyramidal habit of the tree as it grows under cultivation in the Brooklyn Botanic Garden.

Louis Buhle

off; the aim should be to form a neat dwarf bonsai with low short branches.

Trimming of branches—removing or shortening them, or any cutting that causes a wound—should be done in the autumn, when the new growth is hardened. If trimming is done in the spring, when the sap has begun to flow, the sap will come out of the cut end, and the branch will die and may cause the loss of the tree.

If the branches are cut back to some extent when they are hardened, new growth comes out soon. If this cutting is repeated every year, nice bonsai can be formed in a few years.

Watering. Placing the bald cypress bonsai in a basin of water in the spring and summer is good for the tree and also helpful to the grower because then it does not need watering every day.

Repotting is done once in two or three years.

Seeds. Every year I try to raise bald cypress from seeds matured on near-by trees, but only one or two seedlings come up from all the seeds contained in a cone. If viable seeds are plentifully obtainable, I think it is better to raise bald cypress bonsai from seedlings.

59

JAPANESE ZELKOVA BONSAI FROM SEEDLINGS*

How to raise the gray-barked elm from seed and how to train the trees to form miniatures of the naturally grown forest trees

Sinkichi Kano

MY prime objective in growing zelkova bonsai is to reproduce the image of Japanese zelkova (*Zelkova serrata,* or *Z. keaki*) which I have held in mind since early days when I was deeply impressed by these giant trees. Reproduction in miniature of the natural shape and appearance of the old trees is my purpose.

First Year

Sowing. The seed is sown in the spring (late March or early April). Outdoor sowing is satisfactory, but if one wishes to have only thirty to fifty seedlings for bonsai, it is better to sow the seed in a shallow pan, somewhat deeper than the usual growing pans. To provide good

---

*For this article on the raising of bonsai from seedlings, I have been very fortunate in having, through my good friend Mr. Y. Uchida, the editor of a Japanese fruit-growing magazine, the cooperation of Mr. Senkichi Kano. Mr. Kano has long devoted his leisure time and interest solely to raising zelkova bonsai from seed. He is now growing some three hundred zelkovas in pans. These are from 14 to 16 years old and were all grown from seed by Mr. Kano. Born and spending his early life in the mountainous country near Mt. Fuji, Mr. Kano was deeply impressed by the grandeur of the giant zelkovas which he saw growing in nature and in home grounds and came to think of zelkova as the king of trees. Moving to the city of Shizuoka some forty years ago, he was struck by the fact that zelkova bonsai commanded far higher prices than any other kind. The timber of Japanese zelkova is one of the most highly prized in Japan.

drainage, a thin layer of coarse sand is spread on the bottom of the pan, which is then filled to a depth of 2 inches with loamy soil. This is smoothed and pressed lightly on the surface. Place the seeds singly at intervals of 1¼ to 2 inches on the soil, then sift light soil over them until they are covered. After it has been thoroughly watered with a sprinkling can, the pan should be placed under a tree or in some other place shaded from the direct sun; on rainy days it should be moved under a roof. Germination takes three to four weeks.

Transplanting. When the seedlings have produced two or three leaves, about the middle of May, they should be transplanted singly to small pots. Care should be taken to shorten the taproot and spread the slender side roots in all directions so that they will be well developed at the surface of the soil. Fertilizer is applied occasionally; I use decayed rape cake steeped in water. (Also see page 95.)

First training. By August the seedlings will have attained a height of 10 inches or so; this is the time to place a bamboo cane at the side of the trunk for straightening it, tying the trunk to the cane at several places. To insure a straight trunk, the bamboo cane support is needed for three or four years.

Wild seedlings. If mature zelkova trees are accessible, usually one can find 2- to 3-inch seedlings under them in May

Gray-barked elm, or Japanese zelkova bonsai just after leaf thinning and trimming

and June. If straight-trunked ones are selected and carefully dug out so that the roots are not injured, they are good enough to use for raising zelkova bonsai.

Second Year

Root training. The next March it is important to take the tree out of the pot, shake off part of the soil, and examine the root. The development of the root is the vital point in zelkova bonsai. If the roots are well developed on all sides and all these roots are balanced in size, the the tree is considered a fine one. Such nice trees are difficult to obtain, and scarcely one in ten seedlings is so formed. In most seedlings the roots are developed on only one or more sides but not all around. Such a seedling can be induced to produce roots on all sides by cutting off a narrow ring of bark ($\frac{1}{8}$ inch) at the base of the tree where the new root formation is desired, as shown on the next page. The tree is then planted in a deeper pot, the soil covering the roots to a depth of $\frac{5}{8}$ inch above the removed bark ring. All the branches produced on the trunk are removed as soon as they sprout, since it is desired to keep the trunk clean and straight.

Leaf thinning. In the middle of May leaf thinning is practiced, only one third to one fourth of the total number of leaves being left. After leaf thinning, every shoot should be cut back so that only two or three buds are left. This retards growth and maintains dwarfness. The appearance of the trees after these operations is shown in the accompanying photographs.

Third Year

Root trimming. The trees treated for new root production have roots formed

One of the above trees two weeks later, with new foliage

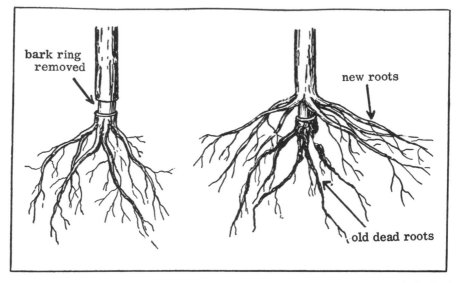

Left: Ring of bark removed at base of year-old zelkova tree to induce formation of new roots on all sides. *Right:* New roots above removed bark ring.

on all sides and at right angles to the trunk, and the old root system is nearly decayed. The old roots under the ring of new ones are cut off and all the new ones are shortened to a length of 2 inches.

Repotting. When the trees are repotted, great care must be taken to arrange the roots as shown in the first sketch on page 63. Unless the roots are arranged like this, the value of a zelkova bonsai is greatly reduced, as the exposed old roots are a primary object of appreciation.

It is essential to use dry soil for repotting, but immediately after repotting, the tree must be thoroughly watered. The pot is filled with water to the edge; when the water sinks away, the pot should once more be filled. While the water is sinking into the soil, the tree should be slighty lifted and shaken. Then the roots will appear exactly as in the second sketch on the next page.

Leaf and shoot trimming. As in the previous year, leaf thinning is practiced. The shoots are trimmed to a good shape and the denser parts thinned out. In trimming, care should be taken not to form the branches as shown in the

first four sketches below, but to try to have them as shown in the last sketch.

Fourth Year and Following Years

Repotting and root trimming. Transplanting (to a pot of the same size or larger) should be done in the spring. Thickly grown parts of the root mass are thinned and all roots formed in the last year are shortened. Then the lower side of the root system is clipped

Left, opposite branches; *right*, one branch immediately above another: both to be avoided in good bonsai

62

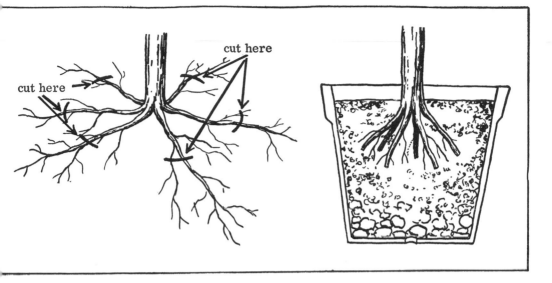

Left: Diagram showing how roots should be arranged and cut when tree is repotted.
Right: Arrangement of roots after tree is watered and slightly lifted and shaken.

evenly with scissors to allow potting and growing in shallow pans. The shallower the pans in which the trees are grown, the better. This transplanting and root trimming should be done every spring throughout the coming year.

Leaf thinning should be done between the middle of May and late June, and at the same time shoot trimming should also be done.

Unwanted sprouts. At budding time in the spring and after leaf thinning, sprouts appear at unexpected places on the trunk and branches, and these should be rubbed off or cut off. Aphids and other insects are exterminated in the usual ways.

Autumn. After the leaves have fallen, any disproportionate and undesirable twigs and shoots are removed, so as to

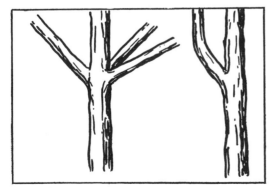

Left, branches in a circle; *right,* branch parallel to trunk: both to be avoided

Branches alternating and spreading—the result to be desired

Winter appearance of a properly trimmed Japanese zelkova bonsai

enhance the symmetrical and delicate beauty of fine twigs and shoots which produce the atmosphere and image of a great tree throughout the winter, as shown in the accompanying photograph.

In the spring, just before the buds burst, for the sake of possible improvement in the beautiful shape of the tree, twigs and shoots are cut back *as short as possible*. Then the renewing and rewarding beauty of the young leaves is awaited.

General Care

For potting soil for zelkova bonsai I use loamy soil from cultivated land or sandy loam from the mountains. The soil is sifted through a sieve (⅛-inch mesh), and used only after it has been well and thoroughly dried. The tree should be planted in the dry soil in the pan, and the pan shaken several times after planting. The surface of the soil is then leveled and immediately watered gently and thoroughly with a watering can. The soil should *never* be pressed.

Surface roots. When a zelkova bonsai becomes older, several roots become thick and appear at the surface of the soil. Such a "root-surfaced-on-the-soil" tree is much sought after and very ornamental. (See page 18.) However, if the roots are

surfaced when the tree is young, they never thicken; only roots in the soil will do so. After learning by bitter experience, I cover surfaced roots slightly with soil, and on this place moss. As the roots develop, the moss becomes scanty and the roots gradually appear on the surface. The trees in the photographs are 14 to 15 years old and the roots are not yet developed sufficiently to appear on the soil. I have several trees of the same age that do show surfaced roots. Bonsai merchants often show surface-root formations in young trees for commercial reasons, but this is not good for nice root formation on the soil later on.

Shading. In the hottest weather, July and August, the trees are shaded; I use marsh-reed screens.

Watering. Overwatering is not good for the trees. However, a zelkova bonsai are grown in shallow pans, they dry out rapidly in the summer, and watering twice a day is necessary; but in other seasons once a day is enough. After the leaves fall in the winter, it is sufficient to give water once every other day.

Training

Materials. For training one should have at hand bamboo cane, string, and wire.

The bamboo cane is split into pieces and each piece is whittled to suitable size for use as a splint for fixing a shoot or a branch in the desired position. The bamboo splints should be tied with string at intervals of an inch or more.

For tying bamboo splints in place, instead of string I prefer the leaves of *Yucca recurvifolia*, an American desert plant which is now grown here and there in Japan. The leaf is split into thin strips and exposed to the sun for one or two hours; it is then just right for tying. If it becomes old and dry, it can be immersed in water before use. It has the advantage that knots made in it do not work loose as do those in string.

If one wishes to narrow a wide fork, the branches should be tied closer together with the yucca leaf. If it is desired to widen the upper part of the fork,

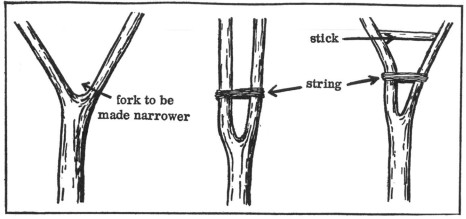

Diagram showing how to change the shape of a fork

a bamboo stick should be placed between the branches, as shown above.

Slender branches trained as described will be well fixed in position in one month or so; thicker ones will take three months.

Copper wire is better than the bamboo for curving branches. A wire of thickness suitable for the branch is selected and coiled around the branch; then the branch is bent to the desired curve. Although easy to use, copper wire will cut into the branch if left on too long a time. Wire should not be left coiled around the branches for more than two months; it is wise to examine it after forty to fifty days.

In growing zelkova bonsai for many years, I have observed many variations in individual trees in the color of young leaves, teeth on the margin of the leaves,

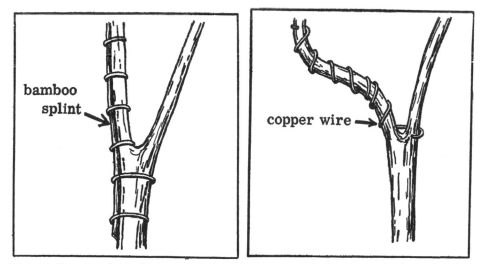

How to tie a bamboo splint on a branch to hold it straight

Method of coiling copper wire around a branch to hold it in a curve

The author and some of his zelkova bonsai

and general form. When they are grown in very shallow pans as shown in the photographs, the leaves become smaller and neater.

Raising zelkova bonsai from seed is very interesting with its growing, thinning, pinching, trimming, and training. No gorgeous colors are produced at any time of the year during the long life of the trees; it is their stature when bare or in full leaf, the aged bark, surfaced roots, and slender, graceful twigs and shoots that charm us so much. Bonsai trees 10 to 20 years old are not yet old enough to give full satisfaction; I think one must wait until they become 50 years old; then at last they are perfect zelkova bonsai.

A black and white illustration fails to reveal the special qualities of the gray bark, clustered bell-like blossoms of spring, and gold and scarlet tinted foliage of autumn, all of which make white enkianthus (*Enkianthus perulatus*) so desirable as a bonsai. From the Brooklyn Botanic Garden collection, a gift of Mr. and Mrs. Howard Phipps.

A few of Mr. Nagao's Yeddo spruce bonsai on growing shelf

YEDDO SPRUCE BONSAI FROM CUTTINGS

How to make and care for the cuttings; how to dwarf and train the trees in ordinary bonsai style or in clasping-stone style

Jitaro Nagao

YEDDO SPRUCE (*Picea jezoensis*) is a good example to show the technique by which bonsai may be made from cuttings, improved year after year, and kept in very dwarfed form within the limited space of the container.

Raising Yeddo spruce bonsai from cuttings is very popular, for two reasons. First, Yeddo spruce is a most suitable conifer for bonsai: it is very lovely and pleasing, particularly in the light green color of the new growth! It is easy to raise from cuttings and easy for the novice to train. Second, the naturally dwarfed old Yeddo spruces from their native habitats have become very scarce in Hokkaido. Whenever particular species are taken from the wild (a pity) they soon become scarce. People do not understand!

My father is said to be the first man who tried to raise Yeddo spruce from cuttings; if I remember rightly, he first tried it in 1913. At that time he was much interested in the *Ishitsuki* style of bonsai, or growing the plant clasping a stone. He made cuttings of Yeddo spruce and they were rooted the second year. After growing them two years more, he then trained them as clasping-stone bonsai. The result was very satisfactory;

67

Yeddo spruce cuttings in propagating bed

hance *clasping-stone-style* Yeddo spruce has become very popular among novices and experts alike.

Cuttings

A good container for rooting the cuttings is a shallow wooden box 1 by 2 feet or so, with some holes in the bottom, or a shallow pot. A little sphagnum moss is spread on the bottom; then the box or pot is filled with sharp, fine sand.

Time. The cuttings are best made in the spring or early summer: in the spring, just before the buds open; or in the summer, when the new growth is hardened. In the summer, only the new growth is used, because it is quicker to root than the old growth—which must be used if the cuttings are made in the spring.

Each spring during the training or improving of Yeddo spruce bonsai, some shoots are shortened or cut off entirely; these shoots are very good material for cuttings. Every fancier of bonsai likes to raise new plants from his own.

The tips of the shoots are taken for cuttings, 1 to 2 inches long; after being recut with a sharp knife, they are inserted quickly in the prepared box or pot.

The container is watered thoroughly from above, and shaded; I use a screen made of marsh reeds. The cuttings must be syringed several times a day for a month or so; this must never be neglected. Or, wrap the container in plastic.

Watering in the summer should be very carefully and thoroughly done and never neglected.

Fertilizer. As with other conifers, Yeddo spruce needs only nitrogenous fertilizer such as rape cake or soy bean cake, while flowering and fruiting trees need more of other elements.

The fertilizer should be applied chiefly in the autumn, when growth has ceased, or after the autumn transplanting. In the growing season a small amount of fertilizer is enough. If much fertilizer is given during the growing season, the leaves become long, soft, and untidy, and strong shoots weaken others; consequently the most desirable or necessary shoots may become poor and die.

Transplanting. In the autumn, say October, the rooted cuttings are transplant-

Yeddo spruce cuttings 2 years old

ed into new fine sand, an inch or so apart. The cuttings generally have two or more tiny branches, and the tips of these branches will touch after the cuttings are transplanted. Sometimes transplanting is done in March or April. In either case (autumn or spring transplanting) the marsh-reed screen is needed for shade, as the young plants burn quickly in the sun.

For a year or so the young plants grow slowly, but in two or three years they show vigorous growth.

Training

Potting. Plants 2 or 3 years old are ready to have their training begun, to suit one's taste. They may be placed singly in containers that seem a little too small for them; or if one desires a miniature forest, he should put several plants together in a shallower and wider container. When a community is thus formed, the branches should be thinned and some of them shortened.

The soil used is a kind that is very porous and poor in nourishment; the subsoil in Japan fulfills this requirement; it

is never enriched; sharp sand is liberally added to it and well mixed with it.

The drain hole at the bottom of the pot is covered with a piece of broken pot; then a thin layer of coarse sharp sand is put in, to allow good drainage. Over this some of the prepared soil is added. The long root of the plant should be shortened. Then the tree is held in the pot with one hand while the soil is filled in with the other and finally rather firmly pressed.

The pot must then be watered very thoroughly. Continued watering must be carefully attended to until new growth appears, and the soil must not be allowed to dry.

Fertilizer. According to the amount of growth, fertilizer should be given twice or thrice in the spring and in the autumn. Rape cake is put in several places on the surface of the soil, or it may be used as liquid fertilizer; for the latter, water in which the cake has soaked for many months is diluted to the proper strength. (See p. 95.)

Time. Training is best done in March and April, but it may be practiced

69

Mitsukoshi Exhibition

Yeddo spruce growing on rock. When on exhibition a layer of pebbles is placed in the large shallow container which is then filled with water.

through the winter, beginning in the autumn.

The desired shape depends entirely on one's taste, of course; but it is better to follow the nature of Yeddo spruce. As good examples to follow. there are here shown photographs of some old Yeddo spruce bonsai—old trees collected in their natural habitats and further trained.

Method. Generally speaking, the most difficult method of training bonsai for the novice and the expert alike is spirally coiling wire around the branch to change it into the desired shape. Happily, however, the wiring of Yeddo spruce is very easy and hence satisfying even to the very beginner. There is only one thing about which the trainer must be cautious. Even slight twisting kills the branches of Yeddo spruce by separating the bark from the wood. Forcibly lifting weeping branches has the same effect. If this peculiarity of the tree is understood and taken into account through the years of training, Yeddo spruce is, as just said, a very easy and pleasant plant to train.

The technique of training a branch into the desired shape is gently to curve it or change its direction while spirally coiling a wire around it. Half a year

Old Yeddo spruce bonsai in rectangular container

or a year later the wire should be un-coiled and removed from the branch, as the branch will then keep its shape without the wire. After they have passed a year without the wire, some of the branches may be somewhat out of shape; these should be wired again and the wire kept on for two more years. Whenever wiring is done, overlapping or weakened or unnecessary branches should be cut off to make the remaining branches healthier and more shapely.

Pinching. In the course of training, pinching of the new growth each year is important and never to be neglected during the whole life of the bonsai. The time for pinching is May and June, when the new growth is $\frac{1}{3}$ inch to $1\frac{1}{8}$ inches long. Half to two thirds of the length of the new growth should be pinched off with the fingers; this must be done carefully to prevent the whole of the new growth from coming off. If the new growth is too hard to be pinched with the fingers, scissors may be used; but finger pinching is better for the plant and has more tendency to keep it dwarf. This is the golden rule of pinching.

When the tree becomes older, deeper pinching should be practiced, leaving only a small portion of the new growth. If it is desired to shorten a long shoot

71

A single aged Yello
spruce reminiscent of
far-away mountains.

to encourage the growth of the branch formed at its base, this should be done gradually, in two or more years, so as not to weaken and kill the branch at the base.

Repotting

Time. Repotting during training is best done in the early spring before the buds open. Sometimes it is attempted when the foliage is well matured; but if it is thus delayed, the new roots will not be formed within the year, and so failure results. Only the expert can repot at any other seasson than early spring.

Repotting should not be needed each year; once in two or three years is enough.

The soil should be porous loam and peat well mixed with sharp sand; various proportions may be tried and the results watched. Results are noticeable in the growth, luster, and size of the leaves, in the health of the roots, and in the condition of the soil—whether it remains porous and does not pack down hard. Such effects will indicate the right materials and the right proportions for the soil.

Method. The tree is pulled out of the container; the old soil is carefully taken off as far as one-fourth to one-third of the radius of the root ball. The roots

Mitsukoshi Exhibition

Several Yeddo spruce trees, 40 to 60 years old, growing as a miniature forest on stone slab

that were wound around the inside of the container are cut off first. Then all the roots are pruned: most of them not so far back as at the last pruning, but some of them farther back; this will keep the healthy roots within the dimensions of the container.

If the plants are to be grown in shallower containers, the lower roots should be cut off, and the upper and surface roots encouraged. Gradually the old tree can be grown in a very shallow container in a healthy condition.

The tree should be repotted in the container and new soil filled in. A stick may be used to poke the soil into contact with the roots. Water should be given just until it drops from the hole in the bottom. For illustrated details see p. 24-26.

Clasping a Stone

Yeddo spruce is very easy to train in *Ishitsuki* style, or clasping-stone style, as mentioned before. To begin with, suitable stones should be obtained. Whenever the bonsai fancier is on a trip, well formed stones will attract his attention.

Time. The clasping operation should be done generally in the spring or autumn; but winter is not a bad season if it is not too severe.

Number of trees. After a stone is selected, one should consider how many trees may be suitably planted on it, and how many crevices it has that are favorable for the roots. One should imagine the development, in years to come, of a miniature landscape which he is creating.

Planting a miniature forest. Each tree should be put into the place chosen for it, and its roots directed downward in a crevice or spread on the face of the stone. The roots should then be plastered to the stone with tough peaty soil. Finally, moistened sphagnum is put on over the soil and held there with wire or string, to keep the soil from drying and to hasten and encourage the growth of roots.

Container. If one desires to place the stone in a container with soil, it is best to select a long-rooted tree and put the farther end of the roots in the soil of

73

the container. If one prefers to place the tree-clasped stone in a shallow basin of water, he should use good enough soil on the stone in the beginning and spread the roots within the dimensions of the stone.

Shading. The trees must be grown in the shade of the marsh-reed screen for some time, until they recover from the shock of transplanting and become rooted on the stone in firm contact with the soil.

Training. In one or two years the trees will be very well rooted and become vigorous. Then the training may begin. Too early wiring would weaken the trees.

In starting the clasping-stone style, an important point to understand is that young trees grow far faster than older ones. One must therefore be careful not to overplant, lest the trees soon become too crowded and out of proportion to the stone on which they grow.

Miniature forest of Yeddo spruce; trunks and branches being trained with copper wire

The wisteria variety Issai is one of the most popular in Japan

WISTERIA BONSAI
How to start with an old plant

IF old living stumps are cut off 1 or 2 feet from the ground, and all the big roots are also cut off close to the stump, the stump can be transplanted into a pot or bed—where it quickly becomes established. When its new life has started scions of garden varieties suitable for dwarfing are grafted on the upper portion. In a few years beautiful flowering potted trees are formed. White and purple Kabitans and pink wisteria rarely have their flower buds damaged by frost. Ebicha and Issai are floriferous and more dwarf in growth.

I raised by layering, some years ago, the two plants in the photograph. The variety is Issai, one of the most popular wisterias in Japan, as it blooms heavily every year, even when young and in pots. By repeated cutting back to the two lowest buds of each shoot, for several years, and by cutting back the strong roots each time, nice dwarfed potted trees are obtained which gradually lose their vine-like habit. In the course of these years, some spurs and small buds are produced. To encourage these spurs to form flower buds in a season or two, repeated pinching should be practiced during the summer growing season. Floriferous dwarfed wisterias will develop (as seen in the photograph). At the end of the growing season, or in winter, all shoots are cut off—only a few promising buds remain for next year's bloom. **K. Y.**

SATSUKI AZALEAS AS DWARFED POTTED SHRUBS

Growing and training beautiful flowering bonsai

Tomisaku Ugajin

AMONG ornamental plants, flowering cherries, camellias, chrysanthemums, Japanese irises, and Satsuki azaleas are some of the great contributions of the Japanese to horticulture. The first four of these, which we have been improving here in Japan for centuries, are now also being improved and are in popular favor in many other countries. What, then, of the Satsuki azalea? In the latter half of the nineteenth century, Satsuki azaleas were taken overseas like many other Japa-

Azalea MINE-NO-YUKI trained as a bonsai. The photographs in this article are taken from the author's book.

For American bonsai fanciers who may have special interest in azaleas: choose varieties with small flowers and small leaves and appealing growth habit to train as bonsai.

Azalea OHSAKAZUKI. This and the other azaleas illustrated in this article were grown by Mr. Ugajin.

nese plants, but I am not familiar with any azaleas from other countries which have been developed from our native Japanese *Rhododendron lateritium.**

Description. Unlike Indian azalea, which has been develop purely for its flowers, Satsuki azalea has tidy fine-textured leaves and appealing habit of

---

*The Satsuki azaleas are derived chiefly from *Rhododendron lateritium,* which is indigenous to Japan; in 1916 Rehder recognized this species as *R. indicum* var. *lateritium,* but all authorities now call it simply *R. indicum.* Some of the Satsuki group have *R. eriocarpum* in their parentage; this Japanese species is now regarded as a variety of *R. indicum.*

The Satsuki azaleas are therefore of Japanese origin, and are different from (though closely related to) the so-called Indian azaleas, now called *R. simsi,* which have originated from Chinese species.

growth of branches and trunk, in addition to the blossoms. It is very well suited for use of bonsai and is the most popular azalea grown in Japan for this purpose. Satsuki azalea generally blooms in early summer, after the young foliage is well expanded. Nowadays, larger blossoms are popular, being 5 to 6 inches in diameter in such varieties as BANJO, BANKWA, GETTOKU, TAIHEI, and BANJO-NO-TSUKI. Some have flowers narrow-petaled, curiously shaped, double, or hose-in-hose (with one corolla within another). Striped, bordered, and white-based blossoms in purplish crimson, other purplish shades, pink, and similar colors are much admired in Japan. Satsuki azalea is most highly developed and appreciated in Utsunomiya (a city not far from Tokyo), where I live and grow it, and in the adjacent districts.

An aged bonsai azalea from the famous collection at the Brooklyn Botanic Garden, gift of Mr. and Mrs. Howard Phipps

Buhle

Culture

If the plants are in unhealthy condition because of overfertilizing, decaying roots, etc., reduce the amount of leaf mold when preparing the soil for repotting. Before being used, the mixed soil should be sorted into two or three grades differing in size of particles, by sifting through sieves having meshes of various sizes. If it is divided into two grades, the coarser-grained should be placed in the container first, filling it two thirds from the bottom, with the remaining third filled with the finer-grained soil. If three grades are used, the coarsest should be used for the bottom third of the container, the medium grade for the middle third, and the remainder filled with the finest grained soil. Finely pulverized soil should never be used; the smallest soil particles should be removed by sifting, and thrown away before the soil is mixed. (See pages 93-94.)

Repotting is best done just after flowering—late May to early June in temperate regions. It is also sometimes done in spring, before the buds burst. Autumn repotting is not so good. It is not necessary to repot every year, but only when the plants are found to be potbound.

The fertilizers used mostly are soy bean cake, rape cake, and dried fish (herring cake, etc.). These are pulverized and placed on the surface of the soil in the container, a small quantity once or twice every month. These fertilizers should be mixed in varying proportions according to the age of the plants and the season in which they are applied. (For more data on fertilizers, see page 95.) Liquid fertilizers are simplest.

Water is given to young plants three or four times a day in spring, summer, and autumn; to old plants, twice a day, in the morning and in the evening. In warm weather it is good to syringe the plants.

Exposure. A sunny and well ventilated place is the best for growing Satsuki azaleas, but in the height of summer they should be in partial shade; I place them under a marsh-reed screen. The more they are exposed to the sun, the better they grow and the thicker the trunk and branches become; therefore to the extent that one can afford the time and effort, they should be watered liberally in order that they may thrive even under the hottest sun. With the approach of freezing weather (in November most generally), keep them in a sunny place and prepare the frost cover.

Propagation. Satsuki azaleas for bonsai are propagated by cuttings. When the young shoots attain a length of 2½ to

Azalea KODAI-NISHIKI

Azalea SATSU-MA-BENI

4 inches and are somewhat hardened (that is in May or June), the shoots are cut off, a few leaves at the bases removed, and the bases recut on a slant and placed in water for two or three hours. These should then be inserted 1 to 2 inches apart and an inch or so deep into a good rooting medium in a cutting box. Water, let drain, and wrap box in polyethylene film. Place in full light (no sun) where they should root in 30 to 40 days. After remaining for fifteen to twenty more days in the cutting boxes or pans, they should be transplanted into soil prepared as described above for young plants. Two weeks or so after this, fertilizer is placed on the soil to encourage growth. If liquid fertilizer is preferred, it must be very dilute, otherwise the fibrous roots often become demaged and may decay.

Training the Plants

Forms. Training Satsuki azaleas as bonsai is most interesting. The forms

79

Azalea Hino-tsukasa

into which they are trained vary according to one's taste and the nature and shape of the plants used. Some of the popular forms are upright single-trunked, upright two-trunked, cascade, several-trunked, several plants potted together, and clasping-stone style. All the training should be carried out gradually, giving consideration to the nature of the azaleas and one's taste. The best times to practice training are just before or just after flowering or from mid-September to October. If training is done in the earlier season, the branches will be fixed and the plants can be released from the copper wire coils in the autumn.

Wire. Six or seven kinds of copper wire are used, selected from No. 1 to No. 23, according to the thickness of the trunk and branches. The wire is well burned in a rice-straw or wheat-straw fire before being used.

Starting the training. It is better to start the training while the azaleas are young, say 3 to 4 years from cuttings, or ⅓ inch or so in diameter at the trunk. In these azaleas it is not difficult to curve the trunk as one wishes, coiling No. 10 copper wire around it. To the branches No. 12 to No. 20 wire is applied, according to their thickness. The copper wire should never be coiled around the trunk and branches too tightly, as it may damage or even kill them. As a precaution the trunk and branches may be covered with hemp fiber before training with the copper wire. If bending at an acute angle is desired, great care must be taken, as breaking will easily occur at the point of bending.

Trimming. All Satsuki azalea bonsai should be trimmed just after flowering, as the new growth breaks the harmony of form or becomes too dense, or shoots that are too strong are produced. If such undesirable growths are cut off or shortened, other new growth may be produced at the point of cutting, and if they are not produced too late, they will form flower buds.

Greenhouse plants. Young azaleas grown in the greenhouse are easier to train into any desired shape and to bend sharply. Old azaleas are brittle.

Aims. Satsuki azalea bonsai fanciers can be divided roughly into two classes: one group appreciates chiefly the styles and shapes of the plants themselves; the other is interested mainly in the blossoms. The latter group can be again divided into two; some of them are interested in the size of the individual blossoms, the others in the colors and markings of the flowers.

To really appreciate the styles and forms of the shrubs, one must have aged and well trained plants, and so Satsuki azalea bonsai have not become every man's hobby. However, starting with several year-old branched plants obtained from nurseries or raised by yourself from cuttings, you can easily train them and in a few years obtain very nice dwarfed plants, tastefully branched. In the course of training these, you will find much of interest and enjoyment.

An amateur bonsai fancier at work among the dwarfed trees in his back yard

THE AMATEUR BONSAI FANCIER

*Something about the tradition and spirit of bonsai,
and what the amateur can accomplish*

Kan Yashiroda

History of Bonsai

IN A remote age, some workaday person or some great genius who was very impressionable and artistic must have been moved by the great beauty and loveliness of nature and must have felt deep peace of mind when imbued with that atmosphere. In the first flush of this feeling, the idea must have come into his mind to copy some of the beauties of nature, in miniature, in containers—in other words, to create *bonsai,* or dwarfed potted plants.

The oldest authentic record of bonsai is pictures of dwarfed trees and herbaceous plants in containers in a noted scroll written in 1310. Through the long are of the civil wars in Japan the cults of nature-bonsai, flower arrangement, and tea ceremony became deep-rooted in average men and great heroes alike.

Then came the **Tokugawa Era.** Turning the leaves of old Japanese gardening books published in the seventeenth and eighteenth centuries, I often came across illustrations and descriptions of bonsai. From these I am convinced that the people of that time were very skillful in dwarfing and training plants and that they had great desire to find new kinds of plants that could be dwarfed successfully.

The accompanying photograph of winter daphne (*D. odora*) is reproduced from a book published in 1827; it shows a crested branch which was rooted as a cutting and perpetuated and trained as a bonsai.

The second photograph is reproduced from a book published in 1837. The first glance shows merely a completed bonsai; but closer inspection reveals that on each branch of the thread-form Sawara cypress (*Chamaecyparis pisifera filifera*) one to three scions of Hiba arbor-vitae, or false arbor-vitae (*Thujopsis dolabrata*), have been grafted. When the graft unions are completed, all the branches of Sawara cypress are to be cut off and the whole tree converted into Hiba arbor-vitae.

These are not childish attempts or vague ideas but are the products of long years of an age of military ascendency, when every profession was hereditary— the time called the Tokugawa Era. In those wonderful long peaceful years, the Japanese people were accustomed to escape from daily life into something that interested them; they devoted their leisure time to things that freed them from the restraint of social life; they entered into friendly rivalry with their fellow fanciers or tried to surprise them in some way. Hence improvement, discovery, and skill in the art of bonsai were much advanced by amateur fanciers. When amateurs have their enthusiasm aroused, they are always without regard for the gain or loss in-

volved; that attitude greatly advanced bonsai.

Professional men have been interested only in seizing the cream of the amateurs' discoveries in ideas and in materials. Therefore I praise the amateur bonsai fancier. In Japan there are nearly as many amateurs as bonsai trees. A large number of them are worthy of saying, as did G. K. Chesterton, "We wear proudly the name of amateur."

Example of an Amateur

As an example of an enthusiastic amateur bonsai fancier, I will tell you of a Mr. Watanabe of the city of Takamatsu, a place noted for bonsai and cage-bird fanciers.

Mr. Watanabe is a salaried man, past middle age. Since the time in his youth when he worked in the Takamatsu post office, he had been enthusiastic about bonsai as a hobby and had built up a varied and interesting collection. Then on a hot summer day in 1945 his house and all his collection were burned and completely destroyed by bombing. A few blank years passed. Gradually, relieving him from self-abandonment, his enthusiasm for bonsai revived and crept back into him. The photograph on page 81 shows part of the result. Beyond the bonsai shelves can be seen a field of grass where dwelling houses once stood in rows. The only other visible sign of the influence of war is several rows of barbed wire encircling the bonsai to protect them from the mischief of passers-by. In taking the pictures I was very careful to keep the wire out of sight as much as possible. "Everybody has come back nearly to the standard of bygone days in clothes, but why not in morale and in taste?" he complained to me, not hatefully or scornfully, but regretfully.

The mental effect that force had, has remained in many cases. However, I have come across young men who are planning to gain refined taste and pleasure by growing bonsai. Some Americans living in Japan also seem to be attracted to bonsai "simply to waste time," as an

American Army Colonel said during a course of instruction on bonsai technique at the bonsaimen's. Doubtless a more serious purpose will be found by many Americans and people in other countries.

Spirit of Bonsai

An old-timer in bonsai (introduced to me by a friend) wrote me a story that has been current in his district for many decades. An American picked up a Japanese black pine bonsai and asked its price, of the farmer who raised it. When the satisfied American had gone nearly out of the gate, it occurred to the farmer that if he said that price was only for the tree, the buyer would pay a little more for the container. He hurried out and asked for the money for the container. On hearing the insatiable claim, the American pulled out the tree the farmer had treasured and threw it to him, saying "I need only the container."

In telling me this story I think my

1837 print. See preceding page.

1827 print. See preceding page.

friend has kindly warned me of the difficulty of making known the *spirit* of bonsai. Whether or not it is possible to convey the *spirit* of noble bonsai raised by worthy growers, it should be easy to describe the technique generally practiced in Japan and to transmit some appreciation of dwarfed trees. It should be possible for the culture of bonsai to be practiced and enjoyed in other countries, and to be adapted in one way or another to the life there.

Since we were beaten in the war and Americans have come in and shown interest in bonsai, some young Japanese bonsai growers are representing themselves as *artists* and bonsai raising as strictly an *art*. If this is so, it is not necessary to use the words "artist" and "art"! This is the last thing that comes to the amateur's mind. The amateurs are generally far richer in culture and talent than the men who cry out that they are artists of bonsai. Possibly the real *spirit* of the cult of bonsai is passed down from father to son, even though amateur bonsai fanciers often show amateurish and poor attempts at growing and training bonsai.

Kinds of Bonsai

There is a wide range of rank among bonsai. One can easily distinguish a mere potted plant from a noble old bonsai; but there are many gradations between the two and there is no strict rule to draw a line between them. Sometimes it is impossible to say which is which—as with the man and the pig in George Orwell's *Animal Farm*.

On mound of soil. The amateur's so-called amateurish efforts in attempting bonsai in unusual ways or according to his own ideas are always associated with his daily life, since reward in money is the least consideration to him; thus they give him endless pleasure, though they may seem childish to the orthodox grower. Such an attempt in Mr. Watanabe's collection is the seedlings of Japanese black pine grown in the mound of soil on an old tile. For a few years after the bombing, the ground in practically the whole city was covered with tiles like this one. The bonsai was started by sowing the pine seeds directly on the mound.

Ever since they were very young, the little trees have been cut back or pinched off repeatedly and severely, and their long needles cut in half. Now it looks very nice; and when it has grown only a few years more, no one could call it a childish effort—as he might do now without knowing the aim.

Various conifers and many other kinds of trees are grown and trained nicely in this novel way, starting from seed. In trying these one may pinch and cut back to his heart's content; **for a man of discernment will find something to be treated with finger nail or shears** almost every day in the course of a year.

It is often said that the best means of controlling temper is to sit down before one's favorite seedling bonsai-in-the-making and trim it to one's satisfaction. I know quite well that there is some truth in this, as I have thus disciplined myself sometimes. This shows that repeated and sometimes very deep cutting back are necessary, to make these seedlings dwarf and finely shaped.

The soil mixture and other materials to make the mound are an interesting problem. One must consider the nature and behavior of the trees sown in it and grown on it; the color, to harmonize with the surroundings; the shape of the mound; water-holding quality and drainage; sunshine, rainfall, wind, drought,

Japanese black pines (*Pinus thunbergi*) raised from seeds sown directly on a mound of soil on a tile

84

Pitch pine (*Pinus rigida*) collected from the sandy wastes of New Jersey. Stubs of dead branches allowed to remain. Tree was grown in 10-inch deep wooden container for 5 years, then root-pruned and transplanted to the present authentic container. Dwarf ferns growing at the base are common polypody.

the degree of freezing of the climate, and other such elements. The soil formed by the entangling and decay of the fibrous roots of the resurrection plant (*Selaginella lepidophylla*) is often used in part or for all of the mound.

Original design. Another amateurish attempt is shown in the photograph of the Japanese black pines in the shallow container. Climbing a mountain a few years ago, the amateur found several young pine trees of tempting shape and somewhat dwarfed naturally, and brought them home and tried them in an ambitious way. They still look like very poor things, but the grower is showing confidence in his attempt. How they will improve as they grow older remains to be seen: that is an interesting point in bonsai growing.

Miniature forest. The picture of Japanese white pine on the next page shows an orthodox method which Mr. Watanabe has started, a method of producing a many-trunked bonsai from one tree. Obtaining a small, well branched Japanese white pine tree from a nursery last year, he planted it in the shallow container, not in the normal way but with the trunk laid horizontally, most of its length just under the surface of the soil. The base of each branch is in the soil, the tip projecting

above the surface, as shown in the photograph. The new growth of the year looks very promising, to grow into nice trunks in years to come. On page 15 and 16 are photographs of similar forms, more mature. Each of these photographs shows not many trees but the branches of a single tree.

I highly recommend this method to my American neighbors. All that is necessary is to pick out a few conifers or other trees from some nursery near home. This kind of bonsai is very easy to grow and manage, and it will not be long before a fine miniature forest is formed in the container.

Plants

Flowering trees. In the villages and hamlets in the mountains of Japan, near houses or on the borders of terraced cultivated lands, one often comes across old stunted trees of Japanese flowering apricot (*Prunus mume*), with trunks nearly rotten but with vigorous young shoots. In late winter or early spring the trees are smothered with blossoms.

Mr. Watanabe brought home one of those trees and trained it into a bonsai; he kept only part of the rotten trunk and cut off nearly all of the roots almost to the base, carefully keeping as many of

85

Japanese white pine (*Pinus parviflora*) with the trunk in a horizontal position and partly covered with soil. When the branches develop they will form a many-trunked bonsai. See pages 15, 16, and 17.

the fibrous rootlets as he could. The result is shown in the photograph on the next page.

Soon after flowering is over, every shoot is cut back to two or three buds; from these buds new shoots will soon grow and replace the ones cut off. Cutting back is repeated every year after flowering. Whenever buds are formed too close to the trunk. very deep cutting back is practiced in order to keep the tree dwarf in stature and to improve the artistic shape of the bonsai.

When I was young, I took home from my father's apple orchard some hollow and rotten-trunked trees, sawing them down to a height of 1½ feet or so. I grew them for a season in the garden and then put them into containers. They were nice bonsai; I well remember that one of them was one of my proud possessions. Old orchards of deciduous fruit trees are rich and profitable places to procure materials for bonsai. Crab apple (page 57) and species of *Malus* used as stocks and found remaining in unproductive orchards may also provide suitable material.

Firethorn (*Pyracantha angustifolia*) is much used as a dwarfed potted shrub in Japan. One is shown in the photograph on page 81, at the extreme right near where Mr. Watanabe is standing. Most of the firethorn bonsai look a bit cheap,

but their orange fruits are nice. Americans have a wider selection of firethorns than we have—many old and new species and varieties to choose from. I venture to advise the novice to begin with firethorn, to get experience in training bonsai with burned copper wire.

The **thick-barked** form of Japanese black pine (*Pinus thunbergi*) is called *Nishiki-matsu,* or Nishiki-pine, and is very highly prized among bonsai fanciers. In the photograph of the collection of plants at the beginning of this article (page 81) two trees are shown at the left on the shelf in the background. One of these two is shown separately on page 88.

A certain percentage of the seedlings come true to the parent and are thick-barked. The photograph on page 89 shows a seedling trained in cascade style; it seems to me that it has lost balance on account of the highly developed bark. There is no hope of new branches from the slender part of the trunk, to say nothing of the thick-barked part. Some fanciers bury the whole of the slender trunk, up to the base of the thick-barked part, and plant it upright, as shown on page 88; that is the natural way and unquestionably the best way. However, the amateur enjoys his adventurous attempt; that is a weak point in one who

Japanese flowering apricot bonsai (*Prunus mume*) developed from an old, nearly dead trunk with young vigorous shoots.

is interested in a thing that will take many years to complete, in this age in which many persons are tempted by speed.

The two bonsai of Nishiki-matsu on page 90 are not seedlings but are grafted on the ordinary Japanese black pine. When they were a year or so old, their trunks were cut off very short. After that, the stronger shoots have always been cut off or shortened and the weaker ones left. Cutting back induces the formation of side branches and keeps the trees very dwarf, so that they are suitable for miniature bonsai which may be grown in such small containers as those shown on page 96.

Even when I saw fifty of these tiny Nishiki-matsu together, I could not find two alike, though they all seemed to be in the same style of training and trimming; however, the old-timer in pine bonsai could tell the owner or trainer of every one of them. It is often said "If you will show me a bonsai, I will tell you the owner or trainer." In short, whether one is looking at a work of creative art, or the work of any outstanding craftsman, distinctive taste, style and skill is always discernible.

Incidentally, I should think sweet gum (*Liquidambar styraciflua*) would be good for bonsai. The deeply furrowed bark of the trunk and the corky branches, which are conspicuous in the winter, should be much appreciated; also the persistent drooping fruit heads and the lustrous maple-like leaves.

Grasslike herbaceous plants, particularly rushes and reeds, are very popular as bonsai in the summer; they are not wanting on the amateur's shelves or in his house but are sometimes lacking in the connoisseur's collection. Some of the reasons are, I guess, that they are low in market value and that they do not need skilled techniques; but the fancier will not say so, if I ask him the reason. (A man does not always tell everything.)

What attractive bonsai these grasslike plants make in the summer can be realized only by trying one or two.

To describe the virtues of rushes and reeds I cannot do better than quote the lines of Alice Meynell: "They are most sensitive to the stealthy breezes, and betray the passing of a wind that even the tree-tops know not of. . . . To the strong wind they bend, showing the silver of their sombre little tassels as fish show the silver of their sides turning in the pathless sea."

Common reed, or reed-grass (*Phragmites maxima*, or *P. communis*), Japanese reed (*P. macer*), giant reed (*Arundo*

The thick-barked form of Japanese black pine is much admired by the Japanese.

donax), eulalia, or silver-grass (*Miscanthus sinensis*), *M. japonicus,* and their garden varieties, and some other giant grasses are easily confined and kept dwarf for years. Old clumps may be collected in the wild or in the garden where someone has neglected dividing them; the older part should be selected, where the stems and leaves are short and slender. A clump of suitable size should be dug, with the clod firmly entangled with the roots. Any strong canes in the clump should be cut off. In giant reed, if a strong cane has one or two leaves at the lowest joints, it may be cut off only down to these leaves.

The old dead clump or the clod with entangled roots keeps its shape and holds the soil firmly for years. This dead clump, with only a few tiny living parts, is really what the grass or reed bonsai will be growing on; but since reeds need a great deal of water, the clump or clod is placed in a basin filled with water as soon as it is dug and properly trimmed. The clump is kept in the basin of water and the plant will remain dwarf and be vigorous (though small in stature) for years, with only a little care which is easily mastered by the novice.

Common scouring-rush (*Equisetum hyemale*), Japanese sweet-flog (*Acorus gramineus*), and such herbaceous plants are grown in the same way or for similar effect.

E. Satomi

Group of bamboos (*Bambusa*) grown as bonsai

Bamboos (*Bambusa*) are among the finest of the grasses for bonsai. There are numerous kinds of bamboo. Dwarf ones and those of medium size easily make fine bonsai in the way just described. One can dwarf a tall bamboo by peeling off the sheaths while the very young shoots are just coming up; a sheath may be taken off every day or less often according to the hardness and growth of the young cane.

If the upper part of a bamboo cane is cut off in early summer or midsummer, when it is approximately full-grown, it will become densely foliaged the next year and be better-looking.

An old specimen of a cascading Japanese white pine, collected about 10 years before this photograph was taken.

These two very dwarfed bonsai were developed by grafting the thick-barked form of Japanese black pine on the ordinary black pine.

Finished Bonsai

"Where can we get them?" will be the cry to the commercial Japanese bonsai fancier and to the American fancier from those who are seeking the much-valued finished bonsai. However, such bonsai can be maintained in perfect condition or at a high standard only by a professional bonsaiman of long experience or a fancier who has developed real skill with bonsai for long years. One who has secured these bonsai by accident or by luck will be bothered and will find himself incessantly busy, trying to maintain them in perfect condition. Of course, the objective of this Handbook is to teach anyone with sufficient interest (and fair skill in plant culture), to grow, train and maintain bonsai of merit.

Plants to Begin With

There is a vast field of plants with which one may pioneer in bonsai culture or with which one may play, in the spirit of an amateur. There are, I think, numerous materials suitable for bonsai in the nurseries and on the mountains in America. If one only gathers a handful of seeds in the woods or somewhere, he can raise many nice bonsai in the course of a few years, as Mr. Watanabe has done with the seeds of Japanese black pine. Bald cypress (*Taxodium distichum*), birches (*Betula*), beeches (*Fagus*), pines (*Pinus*), tupelo, or sour gum (*Nyssa sylvatica*), sweet gum (*Liquidambar*), spruce (*Picea*), larch (*Larix*), Douglas-fir (*Pseudotsuga*), and many American trees provide plenty of seeds to start with; or seedlings may be taken from the natural habitats in a way that will damage the forest constitution.

I recall "California Jottings" by the Viscountess Byng of Vimy in the *Journal of the Royal Horticultural Society*. In her most interesting article she tells us: "Walking is an incomprehensible thing to the average American, and to their way of thinking you walk either because you have not got a car or because you are a mildly mental case." However, I have hope, because she adds a story of the experience of some of her friends: "They saw a man walking, and when they reached him found a placard on his back, 'I am walking, thank you.'"

Now if you walk in the mountains, you will occasionally find naturally dwarfed trees near mountain paths, on the cliffs of rocky coasts, ravines, and mountains, and on the peaks of mountains where eternal winds rule. These will be good materials to start with.

Give me to fashion a thing;
    Give me to shape and mould;
I have found out the song I can sing,
    I am happy, delivered, and bold.
    —Laurence Binyon, *The Secret.*

THE CARE AND MANAGEMENT OF BONSAI

The experience of a California Bonsaiman

Kay K. Omi

Watering. More trees die as a result of neglectful watering or lack of watering than any other cause. One cannot overwater bonsai as long as the water can drain through the soil and out of the drainage holes in the bottom of the container.

During the summer and on warm days the tree should be watered thoroughly at every watering. The beginner should check the drain holes at the bottom of the container for the first week or so until the amount of water necessary to saturate the soil is known. When the soil becomes saturated with moisture, water will drip through the drain holes. For those with only a few trees, a rubber syringe fitted with a spraying head does the job nicely. For those with many trees, a garden hose with an adjustable spray nozzle is an effective and expedient method. The spray in any case should be fine so that the surface soil is not eroded away.

Watering should be through the foliage, using a gentle spray to keep the foliage clean. This doesn't have to be done at every watering, but often enough to discourage pests and scales. The tree should be watered once daily or more frequently under conditions of high temperature and low humidity. Under these conditions it would be wise to water as often as necessary to keep the surface of the soil damp. This may mean watering the tree two or three times daily. In autumn and spring and during weather when temperatures are mild (around 60° to 70° F) the tree should be watered completely to saturation at least once every other day. If in a region where winter temperatures go below freezing, and if the bonsai is winter hardy, it is best to place bonsai in a deep coldframe where the soil will not freeze. Even if kept in such a coldframe, the soil should be moist throughout the winter.

Where to keep the bonsai. The bonsai should be kept outdoors where it is shaded from direct sunlight in the summer and protected from drying winds in the winter.

Maple, wisteria, ginkgo, juniper and cryptomeria should be kept in partial shade the entire year for good color. The maples (*Acer palmatum* and *Acer palmatum dissectum*) should be kept well protected from winds to prevent leaf burn. These maples are also adversely affected by long exposure to direct sun light (especially afternoon sun).

Bonsai can be brought inside to be admired for two or three days out of the week under normal conditions found inside an average home, but can be kept inside for longer periods if the temperatures inside do not exceed 50° F at night and the tree is kept watered during the day. However, one should not hope to keep the trees inside as permanent indoor plants. The best scheme is to bring the tree inside on special occasions and leave it outside at all other times.

In areas which have extremely high summer temperatures, it is mandatory that the tree be placed where it does not receive the direct rays of the sun (morning or afternoon). The best type of shelter from the sun is a lath house or something similar which can filter the sunlight. A bench placed under a shade tree is an excellent spot for the bonsai during hot weather.

Most bonsai can withstand temperatures down to freezing and colder. The danger in prolonged exposure to freezing weather is that moisture in the soil is apt to turn to ice and in freezing will expand and break the container. If the tree is to be left outside in winter, one must take measures to protect and shelter it.

91

Japanese sieves used to screen potting soil are graduated, from coarse to fine mesh, and they nest inside the metal drum. Soil sifted through these screens is separated into the different size granules needed to pot bonsai trees. Watering pot has a fine nozzle

One method is to bury the container in a compost which will generate heat energy on decomposing. The best place to bury the container would be under a tree or next to the house where the bonsai will be sheltered from drying winds.

Another method is to keep the tree in a cool spot (not warmer than 50° F) inside the house for the entire winter season. In this case it is important that there are no gas fumes in the air and that the tree is watered. The tree should be taken outside whenever possible during the day.

A greenhouse with controlled temperatures is probably the best method of protecting bonsai from freezing weather. Temperatures with the greenhouse should not exceed 50° F. (Also see p. 39.)

An enclosure next to the house with a hinged glass roof which can be kept open during the day and closed at night is also a good means of providing shelter. The enclosure should be sunk in the ground to make use of insulation from the surrounding earth.

Repotting. Bonsai are transplanted when the roots in the container have become bound. A root-bound condition is one in which the roots have extended themselves to a point where they are no longer able to gain sustenance from the soil.

Root pruning is not a hazardous operation of it is done at the right time of the year and if one is careful not to take away too much of the soil from the soil root ball. One can safely take away one-third of the total volume of soil from the tree (leaving the remaining two-thirds intact) providing that it is done just before growth starts in spring. This means as the buds swell, and just before leafing out occurs.

Once the tree has been root pruned and transplanted, the tree must be protected from freezing temperatures. In the late spring and summer of the year the tree has been transplanted, it must be protected from direct sunlight. This is particularly important if the bonsai has a full crop of leaves.

One should check for a root-bound condition annually. This can be done simply by taking the tree out of the container in January or February and examining the root ball. If the tree is not root-bound, one can simply put the tree back in the container.

A root-bound tree will have roots growing closely together around the outside of the soil ball. Most trees can live in this

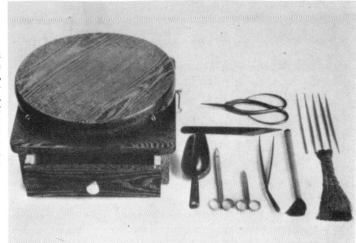

Every well-equipped bonsai grower has one of these imported lazy susans which, with its turn-table top, simplifies the task of pruning, wiring, tieing, and potting a plant. This model comes equipped with b r u s h e s, sticks, snips, tweezers, shears, knife and scoop, which are kept in the drawer

Buhle

root-bound condition for several years, providing that they get ample water. This is an unhealthy condition, however, and it would be advisable to prune the roots back when a root-bound condition is detected.

For transplanting one should have the following:

A. Tools

   1. Four sieves—1/4, 1/8, 1/16 and 1/32-inch

   2. Chopsticks for picking away and later "firming" soil

   3. Pruning shears, knife, brush, wire clipper, trowel, watering can

B. Soil

   1. 1/8 to 1/4-inch gravel

   2. Loam soil

   3. Manure

   4. Leaf mold (well rotted)

   5. River sand (or partially decomposed granite)

     These should be completely dry.

C. Special materials

1. Copper wire and string to tie trees into containers.

2. Moss. This should be dried and powdered.

3. Plastic screen or coconut fiber to cover drain holes in bottom of containers.

4. Separate boxes or pails for soil, manure, leaf mold, sand, and moss.

Procedure for soil preparation:

1. Nest the sieves one on top of the other, with the 1/4-inch sieve on top and the 1/32-inch sieve on the bottom.

2. Pour the loam through the sieves. Break up any large clods of soil on the 1/4-inch sieve and run through sieves.

3. Discard the fine particles which pass through the 1/32-inch sieve.

4. Combine the soil retained on the 1/16 and 1/32-inch sieves and put aside.

5. Process the leaf mold and sand (or partially decomposed granite) in the same manner and put each in a separate container.

Recommended soil mixtures:

Tree Type	Loam	River Sand*	Leaf Mold	Manure
Pine	2	3	1	—
Conifers other than pines, such as juniper, cypress, cedar, fir, hemlock, etc.	3	4	1	—
Zelkova and maples	3	1	—	2
Flowering and fruiting	2	—	—	3

*Or partially decomposed granite.

The figures represent parts by volume. The ingredients should be well mixed before using.

Procedure for transplanting tree. In transplanting pick a day that overcast if you are transplanting outdoors. Transplanting should also be done in a protected area sheltered from winds.

1. Carefully take the tree out of the container without disrupting the soil around the roots. The soil should be moderately dry. Tree placement in the container is important, so when removing the tree from the container, remember where it was placed.

2. Unravel and untangle the roots from the soil root ball.

3. Using a chopstick or pointed stick, gently pick away the soil from the roots on the sides and bottom of the ball. Be sure to remove the wire screening from the bottom of the ball.

4. Remove approximately one-third of the soil from the ball. Be careful not to disrupt the soil around the trunk of the tree.

5. Carefully trim off the roots, now exposed by soil removal, with a pair of sharp snips, leaving an inch or so of the roots extending beyond the soil ball.

6. Before replacing the tree in the container, prepare the container by spreading plastic screening or coconut fiber over the drain holes.

7. Place a layer of 1/8 to 1/4-inch gravel in the bottom of the container.

8. Place enough of the soil mix over the gravel, so that when the tree is seated within the container, the top surface of the soil is even with or slightly below the edge of the container.

9. Place the tree back into the container and locate it where it was before removal.

For bonsai care when on vacation, this plastic tent serves as a moisture-tight "greenhouse." The frame can be made of wire clothes hangers. Water well and allow to drain thoroughly before placing bonsai under tent. Never expose covered plant to direct sunlight.

Buhle

94

10. Fill the sides with the dry soil mixture prescribed.

11. Tamp the soil by repeated jabbings with a chopstick or stick to insure that there are no air pockets around roots.

12. Water the soil to saturation. Always water after tamping and not before.

13. Keep the tree in a shaded location (filtered light, as under lath shade or partial shade of a tree) through the spring and summer when in leaf.

14. Continue to water the tree as you did before transplanting.

Pruning and nipping. Pruning and nipping must be performed on every tree sometime during the year. In the case of deciduous trees, such as maple and zelkova, nipping and thinning is performed throughout the growing season. Do not be afraid to snip new growth in the bud. Juniper, cryptomeria, and cypress are finger-nipped throughout the growing season to keep the tree shaped.

Cedrus atlantica and *Cedrus deodora* can, if needed, be trimmed down to a dormant bud at any time of the year, as long as one doesn't make too many big cuts.

The new growth ("candles") on pine generally is snipped off in spring. About five clusters of needles should be allowed to remain on each candle.

Wire removal. Removal of wire used to shape the trunk and branches usually can be performed after a year's growth. However, for branches of pencil-size or larger trees it may take longer. Wiring and rewiring may sometimes take a great number of years before the tree finally attains the desired shape. In any case, it should be rewired each year so the wire will not scar the bark. When it is desired to train older trees, it may take several years of wiring before the trunk and big branches can assume a permanent bend.

How to Feed Bonsai Plants

Feeding can be performed with any animal or vegetable manure. For most trees, rapeseed or cottonseed meal (vegetable manure) is all that is necessary. Each of these comes in a mealy granular form, and can be administered either in this form, or as a liquid extract.

Application of Meal in Granular Form

This method of application is the simpler of the two methods. The meal is simply sprinkled over the soil. Or, make a thick paste of the meal, and apply in teaspoon-size masses on soil of containers (2 or 3 such masses for each plant).

The meal will begin to decompose on the surface soil in two to three weeks after applied. The first stage in decomposition will be the formation of a white mold. The mold will disappear eventually and with continuous watering, moss formation will begin.

The meal should be sprinkled over the soil about once every 6 weeks between mid-spring and mid-summer. Be liberal in sprinkling it over the soil, but not so much that it will cake.

For flowering and fruiting varieties, one should supplement cottonseed meal with bone meal.

Application of Liquid Fertilizer

Use Fish Emulsion Fertilizer or other commercial liquid fertilizer, diluted according to manufacturer's directions. Do NOT over-fertilize. Liquid fertilizers should be applied three to six times a year, starting as the buds burst in spring, and every three to four weeks thereafter until mid or late summer. Three times each year is enough for pines and similar evergreens.

How much. Use the diluted liquid fertilizer as though you were watering. Do not sprinkle the foliage with fertilizer—only the soil.—Ed.

Bonsai containers are available in a wide range of sizes. In the foreground are a few of the tiniest ones. Those in the background, though larger, are still relatively small, as seen by key at upper left.

CONTAINERS FOR BONSAI

Choosing the proper container for a bonsai specimen is second in importance only to selection and training the tree itself. Since one of the primary aims of the art of bonsai is to suggest nature in its various moods, containers should supplement rather than detract from the beauty of the specimen. Subdued, earthy colors and simple forms are most desirable. Browns, greens, grays, and off-whites are colors well thought of by the Japanese. Some yellow-flowered or yellow-fruited trees are beautifully set off by blue containers. Similarly, containers of deep red hues can be very pleasing with white-flowered plants.

The container is an integral part of the finished composition. It must provide a base solid enough to satisfy the eye, yet must not dwarf the tree itself. Size and shape are as important as color, and "fussy" shapes are distracting and not desirable.

Pottery containers are the only ones commonly used. They may be glazed or unglazed on the outside; but definitely unglazed on the inside. They must have

small holes in the bottom for drainage. Small pots need only one hole, larger ones two or more.

For aquatic plants or for trees growing with their roots confined entirely to soil on a stone, containers should be glazed inside and out and have no drainage holes.

Authentic containers are still difficult to purchase, but Japanese importing firms are glad to help. Whether only a few cents or many dollars are to be spent on a container is a matter of relatively small consequence. But a few thoughtful moments spent in its selection can spell the difference between success and failure in creating a finished bonsai of which one can be proud.

These larger containers are all suitable for bonsai. Their shapes are simple and their colors subdued. They are unglazed on the inside and are provided with drainage holes.